KEY STAGE 2 MATHEMATICS
RESOURCE FILE SERIES

Numeracy ACTIVITIES

Plenary, Practical & Problem Solving

Afzal Ahmed
Honor Williams

NetworkEducationalPress Ltd

© Network Educational Press Ltd

Numeracy Activities
Key stage 2

Published by Network Educational Press Ltd.
PO Box 635
Stafford
ST16 1BF
www.networkpress.co.uk

ISBN 1 85539 102 3

© Afzal Ahmed & Honor Williams 2002

The rights of Afzal Ahmed and Honor Williams to be identified as the authors of this work has been asserted in accordance with Secitons 77 and 78 of the Copyright, Designs and Patents Act 1988.

Layout by Neil Hawkins
Illustrations by Kerry Ingram
Printed by MPG Books Ltd., Bodmin, Cornwall.

Copyright notice

All rights reserved. No part of this publication may be reproduced, stored in a retrieval system or reproduced or transmitted in any form or by any means, electronic, mechanical, photocopying (with the exception of the following pages, which may be copied for use in the purchasing institution: 1–106), recording or otherwise, without the prior written permission of the publishers. This book may not be lent, resold, hired out or otherwise disposed of by way of trade in any form of binding or cover other than that in which it is published without the prior consent of the Publishers.

First published 1997 by Philip Allan Publishers Limited

© Network Educational Press Ltd

Authors

Both authors are based at the Mathematics Centre, Univeristy College Chichester, one of the country's leading centres for mathematics education. **Honor Williams** is Reader in Mathematics Education and Director of Teacher Education. **Afzal Ahmed** is Professor of Mathematics Education and Director of the Mathematics Centre.

The authors work closely with teachers and pupils across the age range and have considerable experience in research and curriculum development. In writing this material, they have drawn on their experience in the UK and internationally.

The authors acknowledge the help provided by Adrienne Quarmby, Watergate School, Isle of Wight, in the process of review and revision.

About this publication

The key aim of this resource file is to help pupils improve their fluency with number and measures. The pack concentrates on teaching skills as well as on pupils' learning experiences. Once teachers become familiar with the content and the approach (see pages 1–7 for a detailed introduction) it should be possible to adapt the material for varying classroom needs. Used appropriately, the units should also improve pupils' confidence in tackling word problems. Some *general* features and suggestions for the use of the material are outlined below. Each unit commences with *specific* operational guidance for teachers.

- Although activities involve individual and group work, whole class discussions can enrich the outcomes. When possible, individuals and groups should be encouraged to explain their understanding of tasks, methods and approaches to the rest of the class.
- Teachers can extend or modify the content to suit their pupils' circumstances by choosing, for example, different units of measurements, number operations or materials and contexts.
- The activities are designed so that answers, scores and targets can be improved by repeating and practising.
- The use of language is vital for pupils to understand and master mathematical concepts. It is important for teachers to support pupils so that they can understand written language and express their ideas to others.
- In some units, the contexts used are taken from outside pupils' *immediate* interests. This is designed to enable them to generalise their knowledge to new situations.

© Network Educational Press Ltd

The units in this resource file are rich in mental activities, real life problems, reasoning and problem-solving activities. The following grid indicates the links to Objectives from the Framework for Teaching Mathematics: Years 4 to 6.

Objectives from the Framework for Teaching Mathematics Year 4 to Year 6		**Unit 1**	**Unit 2**	**Unit 3**	**Unit 4**	**Unit 5**	**Unit 6**	**Unit 7**	**Unit 8**	**Unit 9**	**Unit 10**	**Unit 11**	**Unit 12**	**Unit 13**	**Unit 14**
Numbers and the Number System	Read and write whole numbers, know what each digit in a number represents, and partition into thousands, hundreds, tens and ones.		◆												
	Recognise odd and even numbers and make general statements about them.		◆							◆					
	Recognise multiples and know some tests of divisibility				◆										
	Recognise square numbers.				◆					◆					
	Recognise prime numbers and identify factors.				◆										
	Use fraction notation and recognise the equivalence between fractions						◆								
	Order familiar fractions							◆							
	Find fractions of numbers or quantities						◆								
	Understand percentage as the number of parts in every 100, recognise the equivalence between percentages and fractions and decimals, and find simple percentages of numbers or quantities						◆		◆						
Calculations	Understand the operation of addition and the associated vocabulary, and its relationship to subtraction.	◆									◆			◆	◆
	Understand the operation of subtraction and the associated vocabulary, and its relationship to addition	◆												◆	◆
	Know, with rapid recall, addition and subtraction facts						◆							◆	◆
	Understand the operation of multiplication and the associated vocabulary, and its relationship to addition and division	◆													◆
	Understand the operation of division and the associated vocabulary, and its relationship to subtraction and multiplication														◆

© Network Educational Press Ltd

Objectives from the Framework for Teaching Mathematics Year 4 to Year 6		Unit 1	Unit 2	Unit 3	Unit 4	Unit 5	Unit 6	Unit 7	Unit 8	Unit 9	Unit 10	Unit 11	Unit 12	Unit 13	Unit 14
Solving Problems	Use all four operations to solve word problems involving numbers in real life	◆													
	Use all four operations to solve word problems involving money	◆				◆								◆	
Measures	Use the vocabulary of estimation and approximation; make and justify estimates and approximations of numbers			◆					◆					◆	
	Use vocabulary related to measures			◆					◆						
	Know and use relationships between familiar units			◆											
	Estimate and check, using metric or imperial units			◆					◆						
	Suggest suitable measuring equipment, record estimates and readings from scales to a suitable degree of accuracy										◆				
	Measure and calculate the perimeter and area of simple shapes												◆		
	Use the vocabulary related to time; suggest suitable units of time to estimate or measure					◆			◆		◆				
	Read the time from clocks, calendars and timetables					◆					◆				
Handling Data	Use the language associated with probability to discuss events, including those with equally likely outcomes											◆			
	Solve a problem by collecting, organizing, representing, extracting and interpreting data in tables, graphs and charts											◆			

© Network Educational Press Ltd

© Network Educational Press Ltd

Contents

© Network Educational Press Ltd

The mathematical activities in this file are designed to help pupils:

- gain communication skills – interpreting and expressing quantity, time and space
- understand relationships – describing, comparing, linking operations such as addition, subtraction, multiplication and division
- improve ability to cope with practical situations – shopping, planning, measuring accurately
- become systematic – ordering, tabulating, pattern-spotting, predicting, generalising
- improve mental tools – remembering, imagining, extending
- become curious – patterns , similarities, differences aid curiosity
- improve confidence in tackling tests

© Network Educational Press Ltd

Introduction

Purpose

These materials have been prepared as a flexible resource to help teachers supplement their existing schemes of work. In order to provide a balanced mathematics curriculum and cope with the diversity in classrooms, teachers need to consider a wide range of factors when planning their schemes of work. Many of these are illustrated in the diagram below.

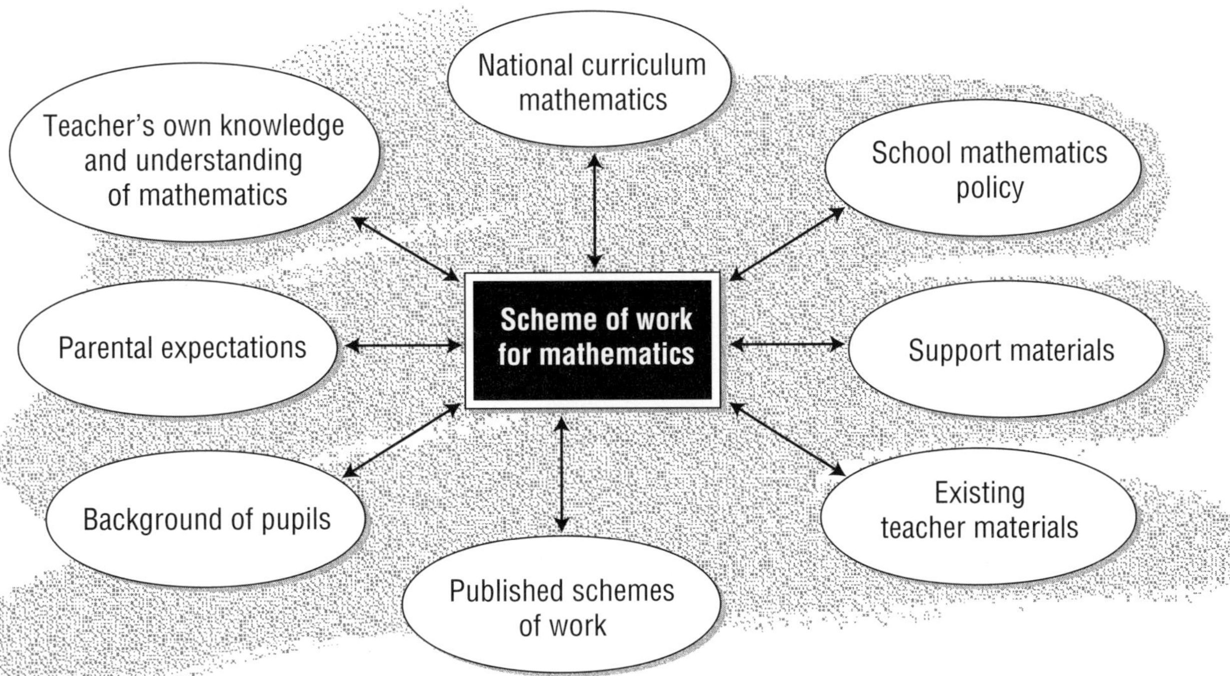

This support pack is arranged as a series of units with both teacher and pupil materials. The starting points, questions and activities are designed to illustrate an approach which would involve pupils in appreciating and understanding the mathematical structures behind the tasks. This approach could easily be used to present other mathematics topics and content to suit particular ages and abilities. The material could also be used as homework tasks to be followed up in the classroom.

The pack focuses on aspects of numeracy concerned with number and measures. The importance of these skills and concepts as fundamental building blocks for further mathematical study cannot be underestimated and pupils should encounter these with increasing sophistication throughout their school life.

Measures The materials include activities which involve pupils in everyday simple, practical and purposeful measuring activities. Estimation and approximation skills play an important role in developing pupils' measuring skills. Encouraging pupils to talk about, record and verify their observations and assertions further aids their understanding.

© Network Educational Press Ltd

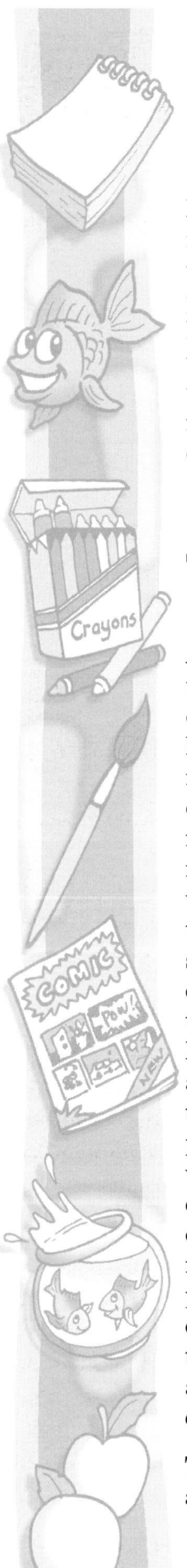

Number Developing pupils' understanding and confidence in formal written mathematical computations is a complex process. It requires them to be involved in a wide range of experiences utilising concrete materials, mental strategies, pen and paper, and calculators. It is important that they develop their own methods of calculating as well as understanding and using formal methods. The ability to determine whether a particular numerical solution is reasonable, verifying mental calculations, using tables, diagrams and graphs, and deciding appropriate mathematical operations in particular contexts are vital experiences for becoming fluent with calculations and estimations.

The units

All schools are engaged in the necessary but difficult task of adapting what they teach and how they teach to the wide-ranging abilities and interests of their pupils. The units in this resource file are structured to meet, as far as possible, pupils' varying aptitudes and perspectives. They are designed to support teachers in a variety of ways and do not attempt to do the teachers' job for them. Each unit contains photocopiable pupil material on a main theme and each activity has the potential to be approached in a variety of ways. These activities can be modified to suit the needs of pupils while maintaining the main teaching and learning purposes. Each unit begins with outlining the main focus, content, notes for teachers, further activities, learning outcomes, evaluation and resources.

Unit Structure

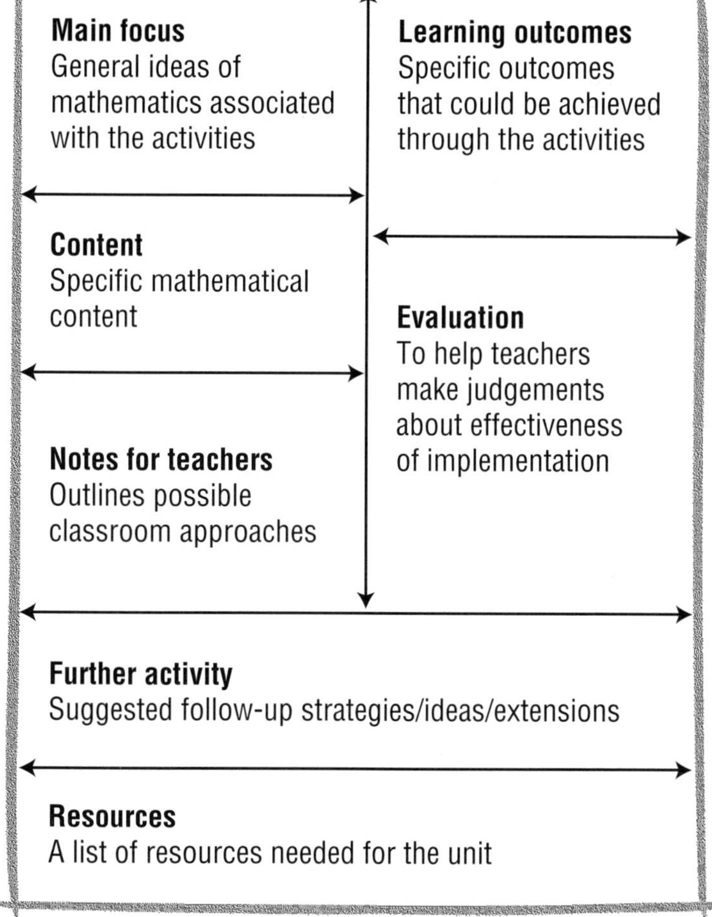

The order of the units is not important. Teachers may wish to vary the order, depth and context of treatment of the units to suit the needs of their pupils.

© Network Educational Press Ltd

Teaching and learning assumptions

The units are based on the assumptions outlined below from the authors' considerable experience in curriculum development in mathematics.

Mathematics learning

Mathematics learning is more effective when it is interesting, enjoyable and challenging. In addition, the following assumptions about mathematical understanding have helped improve children's learning.

Mathematical understanding is improved when:

- pupils interact with people and manipulate materials in a wide variety of situations;
- pupils' experiences are used when appropriate as a source of learning activities;
- pupils are made aware of the relevance of mathematics to their lives;
- pupils are encouraged to use spoken and written language appropriate to their development in order to gain meaning from their mathematical experiences, for example to compose as well as solve problems;
- pupils are encouraged to describe and record relationships as well as to discover and create patterns;
- skills are sustained through meaningful practice and enjoyable drill — this also aids recall of facts and speed in computation;
- imaginative use is made of a wide variety of resources.

Talking, listening, reading and writing

For children to understand, apply and retain mathematics it is important for them to be engaged in talking, listening, reading and writing about mathematics. Language helps pupils to make their experiences meaningful. When they describe or write about their experiences or thinking, it helps them to clarify and develop their own understanding. Mathematical learning is enhanced by the appropriate use of language and, along with symbols and diagrams, it helps pupils formulate and express mathematical ideas.

Talking Providing opportunities for pupils to talk about mathematics in their own words and language is a very important step in helping them learn. Their experience is enriched by listening to their peers and teachers talk about mathematics. Through reflecting, justifying, verifying, questioning ... pupils are able to consolidate their understanding. Teachers' questions can sharpen pupils' thinking and also provide them with a model of how to use questioning to clarify and extend their own understanding. Spending time on discussing statements such as:

'What number is half as big as 12?'
'What number is 12 half as big as?'

is crucial in enabling pupils to extract the correct mathematical operations required to solve problems stated in words.

© Network Educational Press Ltd

When pupils are working from a textbook or worksheet and say *'We are stuck'*, try asking them what they think the question or explanation means. Avoid your own explanations dominating pupils' mathematics. Think of questions you could ask to encourage pupils to extend their own line of thinking.

Mathematical symbols and terminology are a concise form of communication. Each symbol is packed with information which, when expressed in words, requires many words. It is also important to realise that one mathematical symbol may have several interpretations. For example:

14 – 9?

What is the difference between 14 and 9?

Subtract 9 from 14

What would you add to 9 to make 14?

If I have 9, how many more do I need to make 14?

...

How much bigger is 14 than 9?

14 minus 9

From 14 subtract 9

How many more than 9 is 14?

What is 9 subtracted from 14?

Take 9 from 14

14 take away 9

...

Listening Providing mathematical activities which involve pupils in discussions is helpful for both teachers and pupils. It is important for pupils to have sufficient time to organise their thoughts and arrive at some conclusions. When pupils ask questions, teachers should try and resist offering information too quickly without determining pupils' understanding. For example, turn round some of the questions pupils ask you so that they can be involved in answering them.

Developing pupils' ability to listen to each other and to their teachers will help them in:

- decoding the mathematics from a situation;
- understanding key ideas;
- acquiring appropriate mathematical vocabulary;
- checking the relevance of their solutions to the original tasks.

By listening to pupils talking about mathematics, teachers can:

- gauge pupils' levels of understanding;
- ascertain pupils' difficulties, level of confidence and their attitude towards mathematics;
- evaluate the effectiveness of their teaching approaches.

© Network Educational Press Ltd

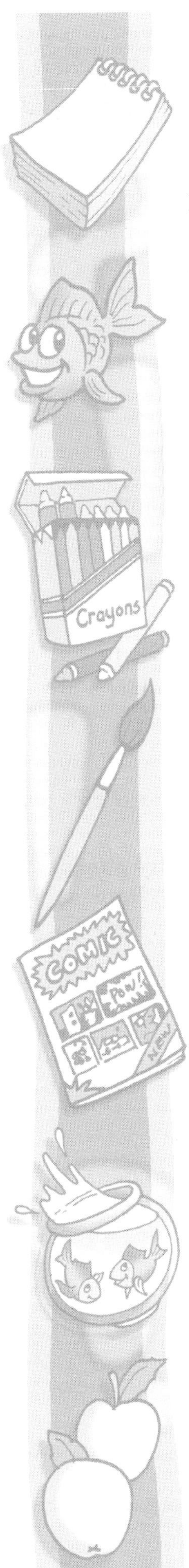

Reading How often do teachers hear comments such as: *'Is this an add or times sum?' 'This is too hard, I can't understand any of it.' 'What do I have to do here?'*

These comments arise because reading for mathematical meanings is not given a priority in the classroom. The difficulties in comprehending mathematical questions are only compounded when pupils' mathematical diet is dominated by activities which avoid words to compensate for real or apparent 'poor reading skills'.

In order to understand, apply and solve mathematical problems, we have to:

- read or listen to the problem;
- comprehend;
- select relevant data and information;
- translate the words into an appropriate mathematical form;
- carry out the necessary procedures;
- translate the answer back into the original context;
- consider if the answer is sensible.

Shortcutting this process by only asking pupils to carry out set procedures inhibits mathematical learning.

Teachers can encourage pupils to read for mathematical meanings by using a variety of materials and strategies:

- inviting pupils to write about the mathematics they do and reading one another's work;
- asking pupils to make up questions around simple mathematical procedures for others to solve;
- asking pupils to decode instructions for model making and games;
- using everyday materials such as newspapers, posters or packaging.

Writing Writing and recording is a powerful means of reinforcing mathematical understanding. It helps pupils to:

- make their thinking explicit and clarify ideas;
- identify different pathways to solutions;
- develop mathematical notation.

It also helps teachers to:

- diagnose misconceptions;
- determine a basis for progressing to the next stage.

© Network Educational Press Ltd

It is important that pupils are aware of the purpose for their writing, feel motivated and confident, and that they are comfortable in using their own words and language patterns. Try, for example, to avoid asking pupils simply to 'write it down'. Create a situation where writing becomes a necessary element for successful completion of the task.

Some classroom strategies for developing talking, listening, reading and writing[1]

- Involve pupils in simple starting points and then try asking how they might vary these or what questions they could think up to answer next. Collect together pupils' suggestions for variations or questions, perhaps on the board or on a large sheet of paper, and try inviting them to follow up a suggestion of their choice.
- Ask pupils to keep a record of questions or other ideas they have not attempted. Encourage them to choose one of those questions to tackle on appropriate occasions.
- Put up examples of pupils' own questions on display. Invite groups to look at and perhaps work on other groups' questions.
- Do not always give pupils rules which work; invite them to try some which do not and to say why they do not — for example, using $n^2 - n + 11$ to generate prime numbers (see Unit 4 and the Case Study on p.103).
- Encourage pupils to find methods and rules for themselves. Try to involve pupils in comparing the methods to agree on the most efficient. See if you can think of ways of involving pupils in generalising for themselves.
- When you want pupils to practise skills, think whether it would be possible for such practice to emerge through pupils' own enquiries or problems which will necessitate the use of these skills.
- Think how you might 'twist' tasks and questions described in textbooks, worksheets or test papers so that pupils can become more involved in making decisions, describing patterns and relationships and testing conjectures.
- Help pupils to appreciate the importance of asking questions such as, *'Is this sensible?'*, *'Can I check this for myself?'* Offer activities which involve pupils in decisions relating to the 'correctness' of a piece of mathematics.
- Show pupils examples of mistakes. Ask them to sort out what the mistakes are and to think how they might have arisen.
- Consider how you might incorporate the terms and notations which you want pupils to learn, so that meaning can be readily ascribed to them and that they can be seen as helpful and necessary.

[1] These strategies have been taken from Ahmed, A. and Williams, H. (1992) *The Raising Achievement in Mathematics Project Report*, WSIHE.

© Network Educational Press Ltd

- Encourage pupils to look for connections between old and new situations, ideas and skills and to ask themselves whether something they did previously might be of use in solving their new problems.
- When a pupil comes up with something which appears initially to be off the track, try to stop yourself from immediately implying that that is the case. What about the possibility of it being kept as a 'further idea' for later?

The activities within the units of this Resource Pack provide considerable scope for teachers to utilise these strategies.

Learning outcomes

All teachers would wish for their pupils to be challenged sufficiently for them to achieve to the best of their ability. The implication of this is that teachers should gain as much insight as possible into their pupils' needs, aptitudes and strengths. This will help in offering pupils appropriate mathematical tasks.

The following questions might prove helpful in evaluating general learning outcomes:

- Does the pupil know and understand what is required?
- Does the pupil need more experience with materials?
- Does the pupil need extension, consolidation or remediation in a particular area?
- Is the pupil making progress?
- Can the pupil apply understanding, knowledge and skills in a variety of situations?
- Does the pupil attempt a range of approaches to problems?
- Does the pupil enjoy the work?
- Is the pupil actively involved?
- Does the pupil offer his/her own starting point/extension?
- Does the pupil communicate mathematics effectively — orally and in writing?
- Does the pupil sometimes achieve unexpected outcomes?
- Was the pupil capable of learning any new skills necessary for the completion of the activity?

© Network Educational Press Ltd

Mathematical understanding is improved when pupils interact with people and manipulate materials in a wide variety of situations.

Involve pupils in simple starting points and collect their suggestions about what questions to ask and answer next. Display these on the board or a flipchart and invite them to follow up a suggestion of their choice.

© Network Educational Press Ltd

Number stories

Main focus

Making sense of problems described in words

Content

Addition and subtraction

Compute with money amounts

Notes for teachers

Discuss one or two problems similar to the pupil task sheets as a class.

Using examples, ensure that all pupils are clear about what they should do.

Ask pupils to do the activity on their own. (*Note:* teachers might decide to pair pupils to help weak readers.)

When most pupils are finished, discuss and compare results. Question 5, on 'sensible prices' (page 13), could give rise to an interesting discussion.

A helpful variation is to ask pupils to discuss and check their work in small groups and choose their best example for a class discussion.

Learning outcomes

The pupils are able to:

- express themselves clearly in both speech and writing and develop reading skills;
- choose sensible data;
- eliminate data not needed;
- use symbols to translate and solve problems.

Evaluation

Could the pupils:

- choose reasonable numbers?
- find correct answers?
- show correct procedures for calculating answers (appropriate to individual pupil's levels)?
- understand standard procedures if used?
- choose and exclude appropriate facts?
- show an understanding of terminology used?

Further activity

Ask all pupils to create and solve their own problems involving addition and subtraction.

Encourage pupils to use sensible data.

The class can be involved in choosing the ten best problems which could be set as homework.

Give pupils questions with insufficient data and ask what they would need to solve them.

Resources

Copies of pupil task sheets, additional examples for initial discussion

© Network Educational Press Ltd

Sensible data

Put some sensible numbers in the spaces.

WORKSPACE

Jack ate .... apples.

Sophie ate .... apples.

How many more apples did Sophie eat than Jack?

Solve the problem and show your working in the workspace. Now show your teacher your answer.

Do the question again using different numbers.

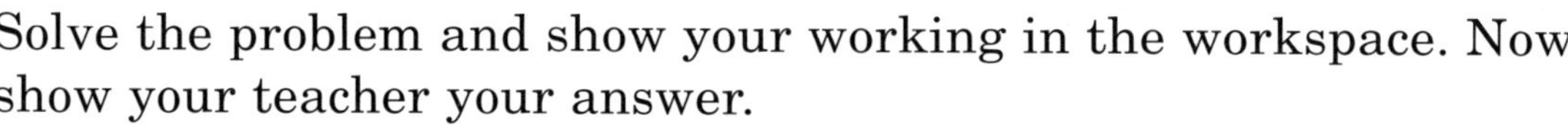

Jack ate .... apples.

Sophie ate .... apples.

How many more apples did Sophie eat than Jack?

Now try these. Make sure your numbers make sense and show your working in the workspace.

1 **I bought .... finger puppets at .... pence each. How much in all did I pay for the puppets?**

© Network Educational Press Ltd

Sensible data

WORKSPACE

2 **Chris bought .... pencils at .... pence each. How much did all the pencils cost?**

3 **Salim weighs .... kg. His father weighs .... kg. How much heavier is Salim's father?**

4 **Jo had .... rabbits. She gave .... of them to Carol. How many does she have left?**

5 **Darren is .... cm tall. His younger brother is .... cm tall. How much taller is Darren?**

6 **Bethan bought .... comics. Each cost .... How much did she spend?**

© Network Educational Press Ltd

Sensible prices

UNIT 1 Number Stories

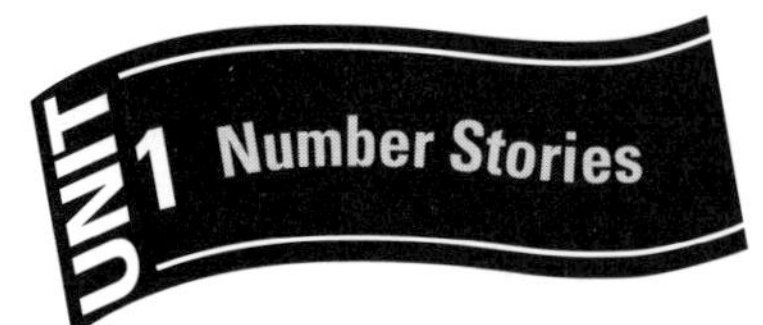

Sometimes the facts you need to solve a problem are given in a picture. Write down sensible prices for each item. The price of the pen has been filled in for you.

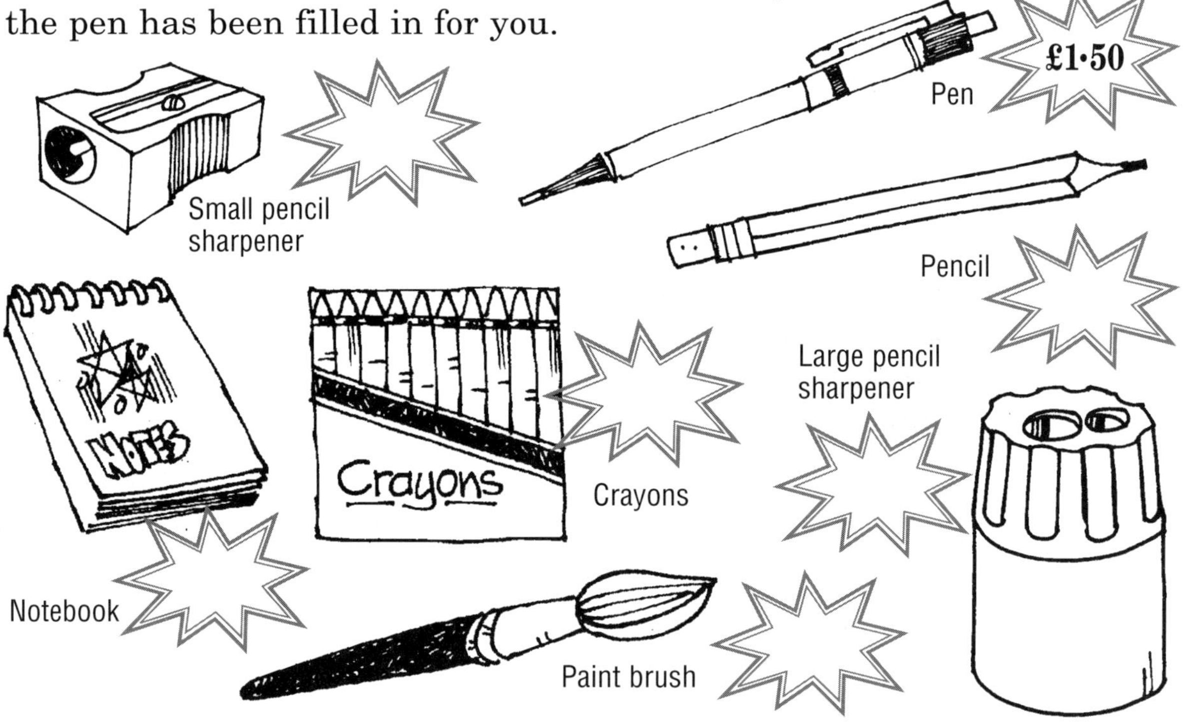

£1·50
Pen
Small pencil sharpener
Pencil
NOTES
Crayons
Large pencil sharpener
Crayons
Notebook
Paint brush

Use the prices in the picture above to solve these problems and show your working.

WORKSPACE

1

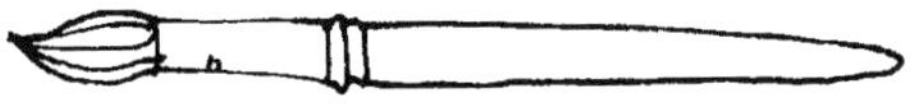

Sue bought a box of crayons and a paint brush. How much did she spend?

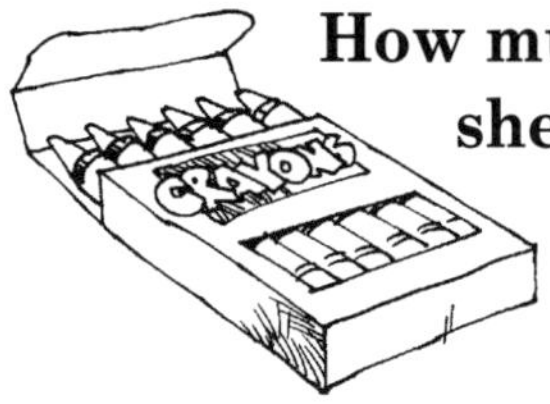

CRAYONS

2

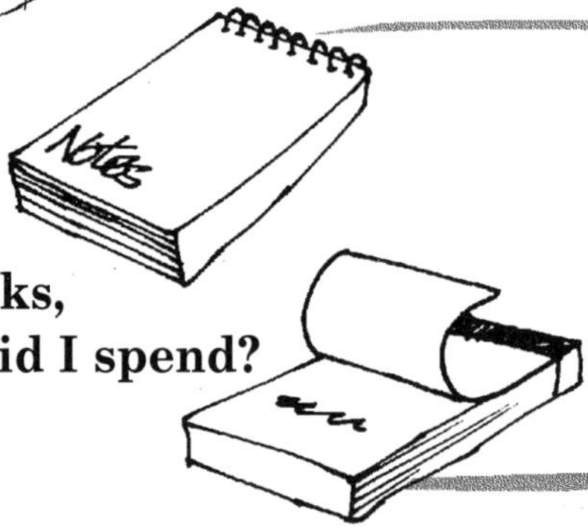

Notes

If I bought two notebooks, how much did I spend?

© Network Educational Press Ltd

Sensible prices

WORKSPACE

3

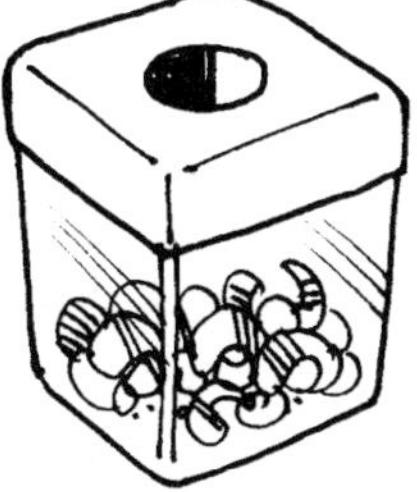

How much more does the large pencil sharpener cost than the small pencil sharpener?

4

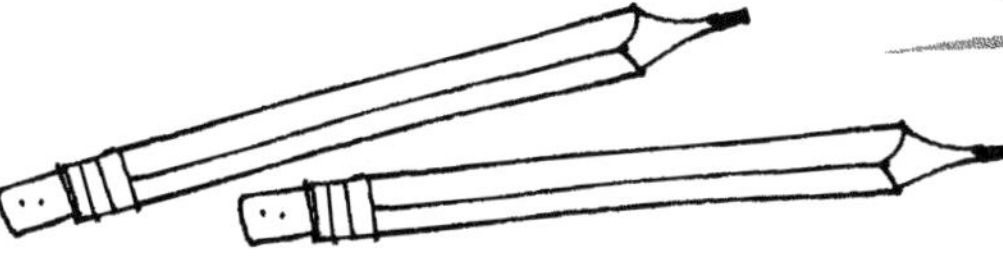

If I bought two pencils and a paint brush, how much would I spend?

5

My sister wants to buy a box of crayons. She has 25p, so how much more money does she need?

6

Donna has £5 and she bought two things. What did she buy?

How much money was left?

7

Carlos bought 3 things. He had £3. What did he buy?

How much money was left?

© Network Educational Press Ltd

The right information

Some problems give more facts than you need. Cross out the information that you do not need to solve the problems below. Then solve the problems.

WORKSPACE

1 **Anna has 16 goldfish. Cathy has 5 goldfish. Mike has a dog and cat. How many more goldfish does Anna have than Cathy?**

2 **Maria bought crisps for 65p and a drink for 42p. Anna bought a cake that cost 85p. How much money did Maria spend?**

3 **I left school at 3.15pm and arrived home at 3.35pm. I had my tea at 5.30pm. How long did it take me to get home?**

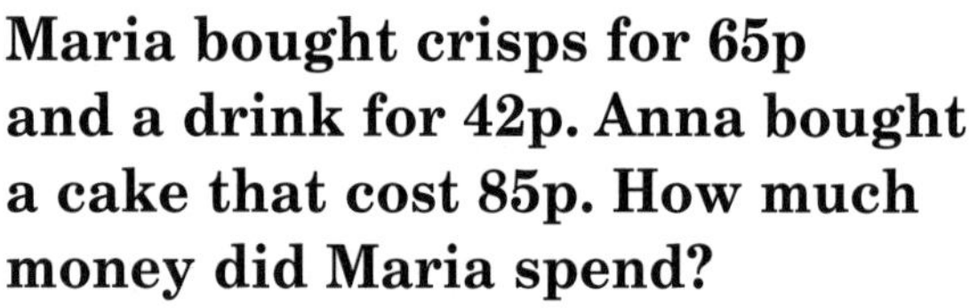

4 **Jamie has £5 a week pocket money. He is 13 years old. Sheena is 9 years old. How much older than Sheena is Jamie?**

5 **In a class there are 28 children. There are 32 large paint brushes and 18 small ones. How many brushes are there altogether?**

6 **There are 126 sheep and 8 goats in a field. The farmer moves 29 sheep to another field. How many sheep are left?**

© Network Educational Press Ltd

Place value in whole numbers

Main focus

Using and extending the understanding of place value

Content

Estimating, recording, manipulating and grouping numbers

Addition and subtraction practice

Notes for teachers

In order for pupils to perform operations with multi-digit numbers, a strong understanding of place value is needed. It would be helpful to consider using one example as a whole class. Although these activities have been written so that pupils can work individually, they do form productive class and small group activities. Class and group discussions help to clarify misconceptions and facilitate understanding.

Special attention needs to be given to zero as a place holder.

All these activities can be easily presented as games or as timed competitions.

Learning outcomes

The pupils are able to:

- read, write and order whole numbers;
- state the place of any digit to a given number;
- place a set of numbers in ascending or descending order;
- apply their knowledge of odd, even, largest, smallest...

Evaluation

Could the pupils:

- read three and four digit numbers written in words?
- match the written numbers with corresponding numerals?
- order four and five digit numbers correctly?
- compare the sizes of numbers?
- interpret vocabulary associated with the tasks?

Further activity

The main content of this unit has been restricted to five-digit numbers, but all activities could be adapted to include larger numbers (additional place value spinners have been included for you to use). Pupils should have a good understanding of numbers up to a million before they undertake activities with numbers greater than a million.

Resources

Copies of pupil task sheets, digit and place value spinners (p.21) to be photocopied onto thin card

Digit arrangements

UNIT 2 Place Value in Whole Numbers

You will need a digit spinner.

Spin the digit spinner 3 times. Write down your digits in any order in the 3 boxes at the top of the left-hand column below.

Using all 3 of your digits once only, make the best numbers you can to fit the statements which follow and write them in the left-hand column. (Some may be impossible!)

Try again with different digits and write your answers in the right-hand column.

1	**Largest possible number**		
2	**Smallest possible number**		
3	**Number nearest to 600**		
4	**Largest even number**		
5	**Smallest odd number**		
6	**Even number nearest to 500**		
7	**Odd number closest to 400**		
8	**Largest number between 460 and 570**		
9	**Smallest number between 725 and 825**		
10	**Smallest odd number between 700 and 800**		

© Network Educational Press Ltd

Find the number

Find the number and put a ring around it in the number grid. Then write it down correctly in the space provided. The one below has been done for you.

7 tens
9 hundreds
2 ones
1 thousand
1972

Now find the following numbers:

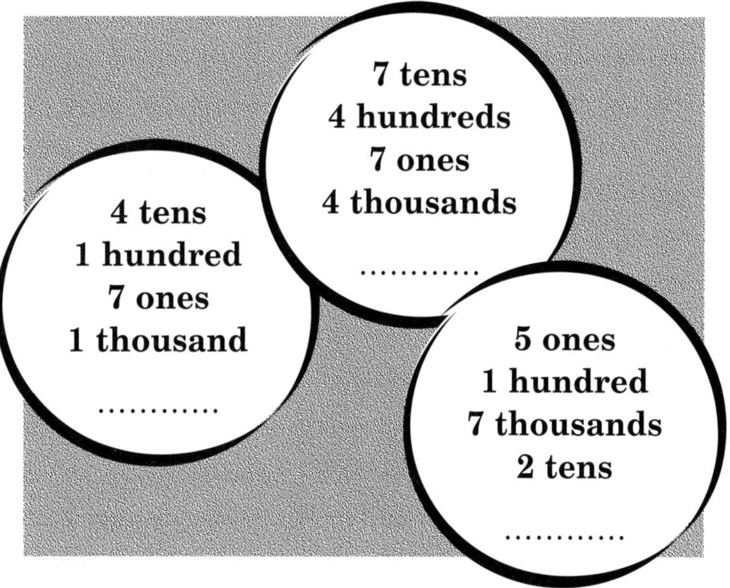

1	2	6	6	1	9	5	7	0	1
8	3	2	5	1	7	9	8	9	7
3	0	3	9	4	4	7	9	3	4
6	9	0	4	7	7	1	8	8	4
4	6	1	1	2	3	2	5	0	9
3	9	4	6	2	7	5	7	5	1
6	0	8	4	9	5	9	3	9	5
4	6	9	1	4	9	0	8	3	2
1	8	3	2	4	7	4	9	5	5
2	9	1	0	8	3	7	5	0	2

© Network Educational Press Ltd

Find the number

UNIT 2 Place Value in Whole Numbers

© Network Educational Press Ltd

Spin and score

A game for 2 or more players

You will need:

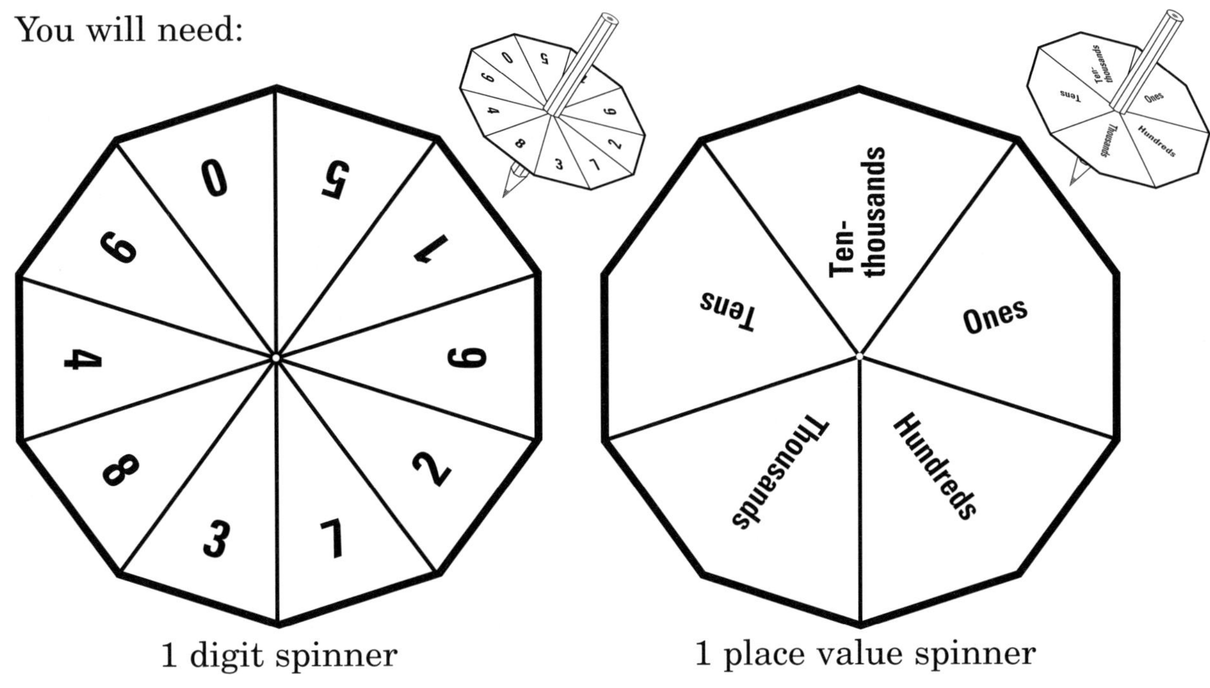

1 digit spinner

1 place value spinner

How to play:

1. **Each player spins the digit spinner. The player with the highest score starts.**

2. **Spin both spinners. Write the digit in the correct place on your score card. For example, if you spin a '7' on your digit spinner and a 'hundred' on your place value spinner, you will write the '7' in here:**

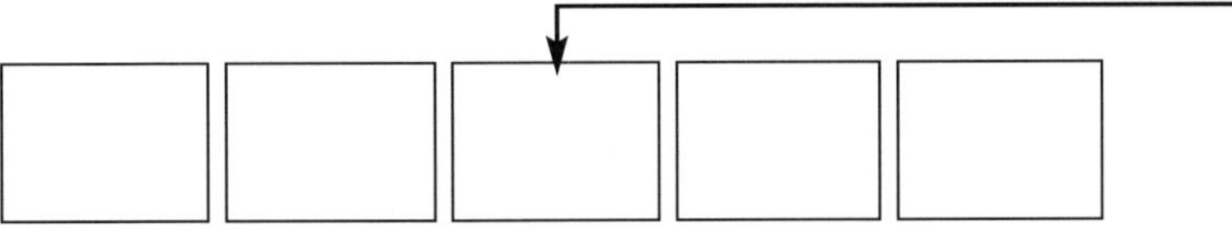

3. **The next player has a go.**

4. **Take it in turns until every space is filled. If your space is already filled with a number, you miss a turn.**

5. **The player who makes the highest number wins the round.**

© Network Educational Press Ltd

Spin and score

	Player 1						Player 2				
Round 1											
Round 2											
Round 3											
Round 4											
Round 5											
Round 6											
Round 7											
Round 8											
Round 9											
Round 10											

© Network Educational Press Ltd

Place value and digit spinners

0 5 1 6 2 7 3 8 4 9

0 5 1 6 2 7 3 8 4 9

Ten-thousands, Ones, Hundreds, Thousands, Tens

Ten-thousands, Ones, Hundreds, Thousands, Tens

Hundreds, Ten-thousands, Ones, Hundred-thousands, Tens, Millions, Hundred-millions, Ten-millions, Thousands

Hundreds, Ten-thousands, Ones, Hundred-thousands, Tens, Millions, Hundred-millions, Ten-millions, Thousands

© Network Educational Press Ltd

Get closer

You will need to use a digit spinner.

Look at your target number.

Using the spinner:

- **can you make the number given?**
- **can you make a number close to it but smaller?**

How to find out

Spin the digit spinner. Choose where to put the number on the grid and write the number down.

Continue until all the spaces are filled.

How close were you to the target?

Work out the difference between the 2 numbers — this is your score. If your number is bigger than the target, your score is 100.

1. Target number **6 7 5**
My number is ☐☐☐
My score is ☐☐☐

2. Target number **8 0 0**
My number is ☐☐☐
My score is ☐☐☐

3. Target number **2 3 4**
My number is ☐☐☐
My score is ☐☐☐

4. Target number **3 0 1**
My number is ☐☐☐
My score is ☐☐☐

5. Target number **2 3 4**
My number is ☐☐☐
My score is ☐☐☐

Total score

Compare your final score with other pupils in your class.
You should try to have the lowest score.

© Network Educational Press Ltd

Get closer

For these target numbers you will need to spin the spinner 4 times.
If your number is bigger than the target, your score is 1000.

1. Target number **2 9 9 5**
My number is
My score is

2. Target number **6 0 0 0**
My number is
My score is

3. Target number **7 0 1 0**
My number is
My score is

4. Target number **5 9 7 2**
My number is
My score is

5. Target number **9 9 2 3**
My number is
My score is

Total score

For these target numbers you will need to spin the spinner 5 times.
If your number is bigger than the target, your score is 10 000.

1. Target number **9 8 3 5 7**
My number is
My score is

2. Target number **5 0 7 9 4**
My number is
My score is

3. Target number **3 1 6 7 8**
My number is
My score is

4. Target number **8 7 9 4 8**
My number is
My score is

5. Target number **7 1 0 0 5**
My number is
My score is

Total score

© Network Educational Press Ltd

Mathematical understanding is improved when pupils' own experiences are used appropriately as a source of learning activities.

Help pupils to appreciate the importance of asking questions like 'Is this sensible?' 'Can I check this for myself?'

© Network Educational Press Ltd

Exact and approximate lengths

Main focus

Exploring the relationship between different lengths

Content

Measurement and comparison of lengths — millimetres, centimetres and metres

Approximate conversions of feet and inches to metres

Notes for teachers

Pupils should already be experienced in using a range of everyday objects to compare and order lengths.

The 'Measuring up' task is best carried out in pairs. The data generated from the tasks can be used at a later date for data-handling activities. The recording of measurements could also be refined through the use of decimal notation.

The emphasis for the 'Tall facts' task is on finding approximate equivalents and not on finding an exact conversion. It would be helpful to start this activity with a discussion on approximate conversions from feet to metres.

Learning outcomes

The pupils are able to:

- estimate and measure objects in their environment;
- select units appropriate to the objects measured, for example millimetres, centimetres, metres;
- familiarise themselves with relative heights of objects not always measured;
- use scales to relate imperial and metric measures.

Evaluation

Could the pupils:

- make sensible estimates of various sizes?
- measure accurately in centimetres and millimetres?
- compare and talk about relative sizes?
- check their work?

Further activity

Pupils could be asked to investigate the relationship between heights given in 'Tall facts' and one kilometre — for example, how many people would have to lie down (head to foot) to cover one kilometre?

Utilise class data to investigate 'average sizes' from the 'Measuring up' activity. The tasks could also be adapted for sensible weight measurement.

The 'Measuring up' activity could lead to projects such as devising measurements for desks and chairs for an infant or secondary school.

Resources

Copies of pupil task sheets, pieces of string, tape measures, rulers

© Network Educational Press Ltd

Sensible measurements?

Look at the measurements. Say which ones are sensible and which are not by putting a circle around the correct answer. If you think the measurement is not sensible, write down what would be a sensible measurement and say why.

The length of a grain of rice is 2 centimetres.

Sensible/Not sensible

....

....

....

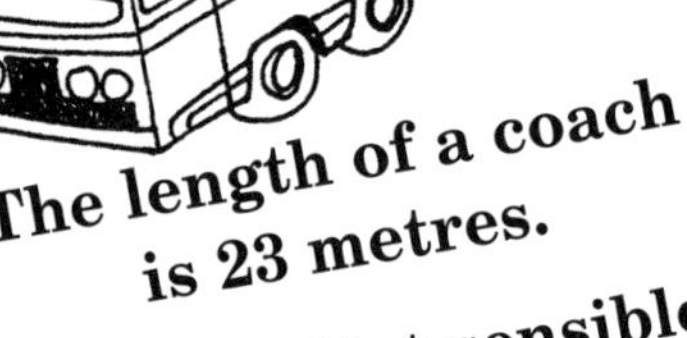

The length of a coach is 23 metres.

Sensible/Not sensible

....

....

....

The Eiffel Tower is about 300 metres.

Sensible/Not sensible

....

....

....

A house is about 60 metres high.

Sensible/Not sensible

....

....

....

The length of an adult's thumb is about 8 centimetres.

Sensible/Not sensible

....

....

....

A blue whale is about 90 metres.

Sensible/Not sensible

....

....

....

© Network Educational Press Ltd

Measuring up

Height of my ear

My guess
....
My measurement
....

Height of a chair from the floor
My guess
....
My measurement
....

Length of a recorder
My guess
....
My measurement
....

Length of a pencil sharpener
My guess
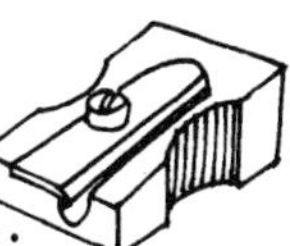
....
My measurement
....

Length of a paint brush
My guess
....
My measurement
....

Height of a desk from the floor
My guess
....
My measurement
....

Length of my thumb nail

My guess

....
My measurement
....

Distance from my knee to the floor
My guess
....
My measurement
....

Diameter of a 10p coin

My guess

....
My measurement
....

Circumference of my neck

My guess
....
My measurement
....

Circumference of my wrist
My guess
....
My measurement
....

Length of my shoe
My guess

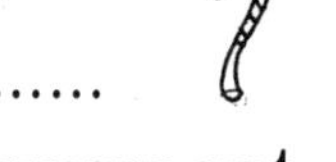
....
My measurement
....

Width of the classroom door
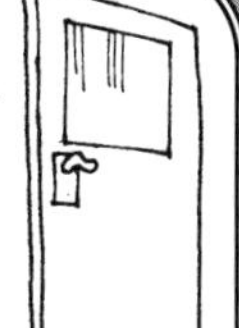
My guess

....
My measurement
....

Distance of the light switch from the floor
My guess

....
My measurement
....

Distance of the door handle from the floor
My guess
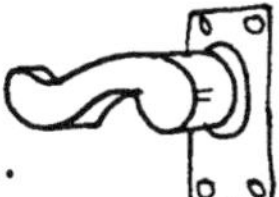
....
My measurement
....

© Network Educational Press Ltd

Tall facts

Look at the scale bar below. The heights have been given in feet and inches.

Can you work out what their heights are to the nearest metre so that you can mark your answers on the scale? (The first one has been done for you.)

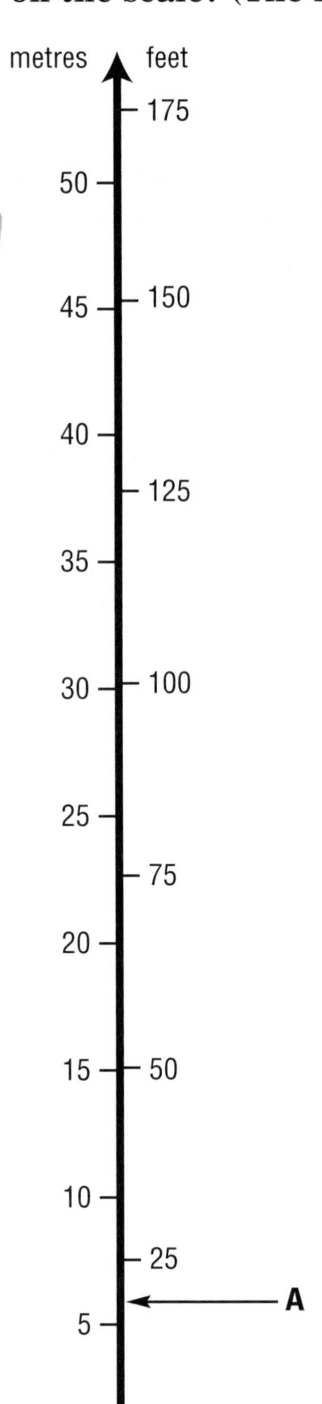

A. Giraffe 19 feet

B. Man 5 feet 9 inches

C. Highest calculated sea wave (1933) 112 feet

D. Highest measured sea wave (1961) 67 feet

E. Giant bamboo 121 feet

F. Horse (shoulder height) 5 feet 6 inches

G. Hot air balloon (height reached in 1783) 80 feet

H. Totem pole, USA 160 feet

I. Smallest house in Britain 10 feet 2 inches high

J. Highest tomato plant (1957) 20 feet

K. Poplar tree 30 feet

L. North African ostrich 9 feet

M. Willow tree 40 feet

© Network Educational Press Ltd

Factors, products and primes

UNIT 4

Main focus

Reinforcing relationships between two or more numbers, especially factors, multiples, primes

Content

Factors, multiples, primes, sum of primes

Notes for teachers

These tasks assume pupils' familiarity with prime numbers up to 100 and methods such as the Sieve of Eratosthenes.

It might be useful to start off the lesson by giving pupils a 1 → 100 number grid and asking them to mark the prime numbers.

This can be followed by a class discussion to confirm pupils' understanding.

Encouraging pupils to explain their answers and rules to each other will help them to crystallise definitions and relationships.

Learning outcomes

The pupils are able to:

- understand the following terms: factor, multiple, divisible, even, odd, square and prime;
- use the above terms in spotting and in writing down number relationships;
- extend mental and written computation.

Evaluation

Could the pupils:

- compute the sum and products correctly?
- correctly interpret the mathematical terms and symbols used?
- recall number bonds fluently?
- express rules in words?

Further activity

Ask pupils to write $n^2 - n + 11$ and investigate the values of n which will give prime numbers. Replace 11 in the expression with other numbers such as 13, 17, 41 to find some good generators of primes. Refer to the Case Study of this work with 10/11-year-old pupils on p.103.

Resources

Copies of pupil task sheets, dice, 1 → 100 number grid on p.33 (optional)

© Network Educational Press Ltd

Spot the numbers

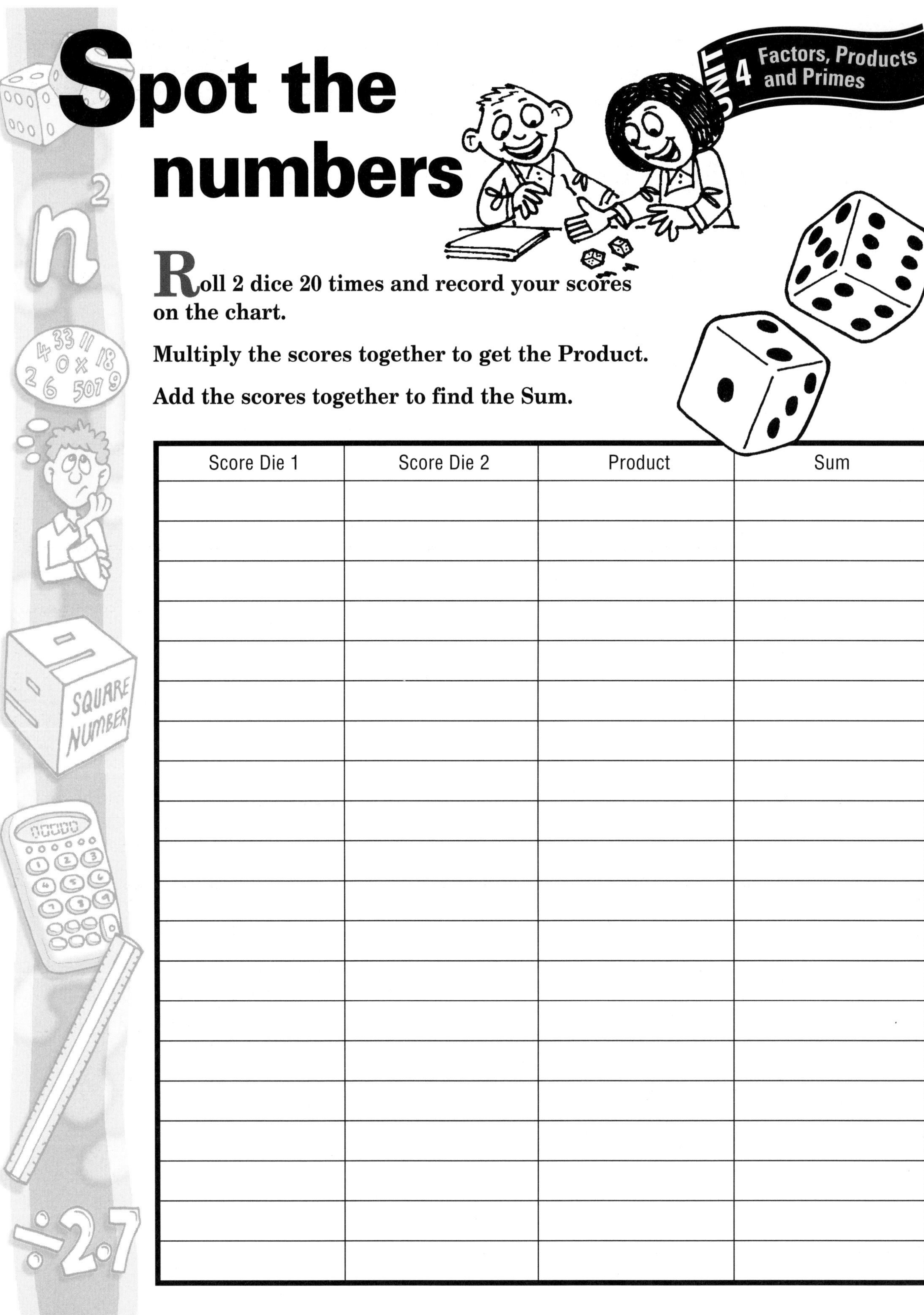

Roll 2 dice 20 times and record your scores on the chart.

Multiply the scores together to get the Product.

Add the scores together to find the Sum.

Score Die 1	Score Die 2	Product	Sum

© Network Educational Press Ltd

Spot the numbers

From your results, write all your scores that can fit these statements. (Some may be impossible!)

Chart 1

The product is less than 10.	
The product is a multiple of 3 between 10 and 20.	
The product is divisible by 6.	
The product is an odd number between 20 and 30.	
The product is a multiple of 5.	
The product is a square number.	
The product is a prime number.	

Chart 2

The sum is > 7.	
The sum is divisible by 3.	
The sum is a multiple of 4.	
The sum is divisible by 2.	
The sum is a prime number.	
The sum is < 5.	
The sum is a square number.	

Look back at your charts. Were there any that were impossible?

What scores would you need to complete the table?

Further challenges

Find the product which has the greatest number of factors.

....

Find the sum which is an even number and also the sum of 2 prime numbers.

....

© Network Educational Press Ltd

Sum of primes

From your product tables, choose five *even* numbers greater than 2. Write each of these numbers as the *sum* of 2 *prime* numbers.

Try to write them as the *sum* of three prime numbers.

My number	Sum of 2 prime numbers	Sum of 3 prime numbers
20	3 + 17, 7 + 13	2 + 5 + 13, 2 + 7 + 11

Try some more even numbers of your own.

Now try some odd numbers.

My number	Sum of 2 prime numbers	Sum of 3 prime numbers
15	13 + 2	3 + 5 + 7, 5 + 5 + 5, 11 + 2 + 2

You might be interested in finding out about the 18th-century German Mathematician called Goldbach and his Conjecture on prime numbers.

© Network Educational Press Ltd

1–100 grids

1	2	3	4	5	6	7	8	9	10
11	12	13	14	15	16	17	18	19	20
21	22	23	24	25	26	27	28	29	30
31	32	33	34	35	36	37	38	39	40
41	42	43	44	45	46	47	48	49	50
51	52	53	54	55	56	57	58	59	60
61	62	63	64	65	66	67	68	69	70
71	72	73	74	75	76	77	78	79	80
81	82	83	84	85	86	87	88	89	90
91	92	93	94	95	96	97	98	99	100

1	2	3	4	5	6	7	8	9	10
11	12	13	14	15	16	17	18	19	20
21	22	23	24	25	26	27	28	29	30
31	32	33	34	35	36	37	38	39	40
41	42	43	44	45	46	47	48	49	50
51	52	53	54	55	56	57	58	59	60
61	62	63	64	65	66	67	68	69	70
71	72	73	74	75	76	77	78	79	80
81	82	83	84	85	86	87	88	89	90
91	92	93	94	95	96	97	98	99	100

© Network Educational Press Ltd

Mathematical understanding is improved when pupils are made aware of the relevance of mathematics to their lives.

Ask pupils to keep a record of questions or other ideas they have not attempted. Encourage them to tackle one of those on appropriate occasions.

© Network Educational Press Ltd

Number cards (4 sets)

Note: these cards have been adapted from *Do Discuss Mathscards* (Blackie Chambers, 1972)

Main focus

Fluency with money, 24-hour clock and percentages

Content

Practice with number bonds, mental calculations, percentages, relationship between fractions and percentages in the context of money

Notes for teachers

These cards can be used for 3 purposes:

- Class use — the cards are arranged to go around in a full circle. A pupil starts by reading aloud his/her main number, followed by the question below. This is answered by the pupil who has the answer at the top of the card. This process is repeated until all the cards have been used. The cards can be re-shuffled and the process repeated. An element of urgency can be introduced by timing the activity. Teachers will need to be sensitive to individual pupils' difficulties and read the question/answer if necessary.
- Group use — teachers may wish to divide pupils into groups according to pace. Working together can help pupils overcome reading and counting difficulties. Pencil and paper can be allowed to deal with more difficult cards.
- Individual use — once pupils have an idea of how the cards work, they can use sets of cards individually. A written record could be kept.

Learning outcomes

The pupils are able to:

- read and interpret mathematical questions fluently;
- understand and work out answers mentally;
- check mental calculations.

Evaluation

Could the pupils:

- read the cards correctly?
- convert the correct time between the 12-hour and 24-hour clock?
- establish equivalence between fractions and percentages in the context of money?
- calculate quickly simple problems involving money?
- verify calculations using pen and paper methods?

Further activity

This idea can be adapted for other mathematical topics or more difficult questions using blank playing cards. (*Note:* see Loop Cards devised by Adrian Pinel, Chichester Institute of Higher Education.)

Resources

Sets of number cards (best photocopied onto thin card)

© Network Educational Press Ltd

Calculation cards

13 Take away ten	5 Multiply by six	60 How many sixes is this?
17 Subtract 4	15 What is one third of this?	48 Add twelve
8 Nine more would be .... ?	24 Take nine away	16 Multiply by three
11 Three less would be .... ?	6 Who has four times this?	19 Subtract three
7 Add four	4 Add two	14 Add five
21 Divide by three	20 What is one fifth of this?	2 What are seven twos?
30 Who has nine less?	10 Multiply by two	12 How many sixes is this?

© Network Educational Press Ltd

Calculation cards

36 How many threes is this?	31 Add six	18 Add ten
44 What is eight less?	22 What would be nine more?	9 Double this
37 What is seven more?	28 Who has six less?	3 Multiply by three

Money cards

14p Take away 10p	30p What would be the change from 50p?	32p What is the cost of 2 bars of chocolate at 32p each?
4p What is the cost of 8 sweets at 4p each?	15p Take away 3p	36p How many 4p counters would this buy?
8p Add 8p and 6p	12p What is the cost of one dozen eggs at 12p each?	9 What is the cost of 9 cans of drink at 40p each?

© Network Educational Press Ltd

Money cards

35p Take away 20p	£18 What would be the change from 4 £5 notes?	£2 Take away £1.50
64p What would be the change from £1?	60p What would be the change from £1?	20p How many 20p stamps would you get for £1?
£3.60 Take away 60p	£3 How many 50p coins does this make?	12 What is the value of 12 coins at 2p each?
5 What is the cost of 5 pencils at 12p each?	£1.44 Take away 44p	£6 How many pence are there in £6?
60 What is the cost of 60 tickets at 30p each?	40p Take away 5p	24p Add 6p
50p Take away 42p	6 What is double 6?	

© Network Educational Press Ltd

Fraction cards

50% Find 50% of £10	75% Find 75% of £8	$\frac{7}{10}$ What percentage is this?
£5 What fraction of £20 is this?	10% Find 10% of £450	20% What is 20% of £35?
£6 What fraction of £20 is this?	70% Find 70% of £30	£7 What fraction of £21 is this?
£45 What fraction of £50 is this?	$\frac{1}{3}$ What percentage is this?	£30 What fraction of £40 is this?
£21 What fraction of £168 is this?	$33\frac{1}{3}$ % Find $33\frac{1}{3}$ % of £12	£12 What fraction of £120 is this?
£4 What fraction of £8 is this?	$\frac{3}{4}$ What percentage is this?	£63 What fraction of £90 is this?
$\frac{1}{2}$ What percentage is this?	$\frac{1}{10}$ What percentage is this?	$12\frac{1}{2}$ % Find $12\frac{1}{2}$ % of £72

© Network Educational Press Ltd

Fraction cards

$\frac{1}{5}$ What percentage is this?	90% Find 90% of £70	$\frac{1}{4}$ What percentage is this?
25% Find 25% of £120	$\frac{1}{8}$ What percentage is this?	$\frac{3}{10}$ What percentage is this?
30% Find 30% of £40	£9 What fraction of £45 is this?	$\frac{9}{10}$ What percentage is this?

Time cards

3pm What is the time 12 hours later — 3am or 3pm?	10.30am What is the time 30 minutes later?	2pm What is the time 30 minutes earlier?
1pm What is the time 15 minutes earlier?	3am What is the time 7 hours later?	10am What is the time 12 hours later?
Midnight What is the time 8½ hours later?	12.30pm What is the time 45 minutes later?	1.30pm What is the time 30 minutes earlier?

© Network Educational Press Ltd

Time cards

10pm What is the time 2 hours later?	**11.45am** What is the time 1 hour earlier?	**2.30pm** What is this on the 24-hour clock?
1.15pm What is the time 45 minutes later?	**10.45am** What is the time ½ hour earlier?	**11am** What is the time 1½ hours later?
9.00am What is the time 1 hour earlier?	**2400 hours (midnight)** How many hours for midday on the 24-hour clock?	**10.15am** What is the time ½ hour earlier?
9.45am What is the time ¾ hour earlier?	**2030 hours** What is the time ½ hour later on the 24-hour clock?	**8am** What is the time 6½ hours later?
2100 hours What is the time 3 hours later on the 24-hour clock?	**14.30 hours** What is the time 3½ hours later on the 24-hour clock?	**12.45pm** What is the time 1 hour earlier?
2000 hours What is the time ½ hour later on the 24-hour clock?	**1200 hours** What is the time 3 hours later — 3am or 3pm?	
1800 hours What is the time 2 hours later on the 24-hour clock?	**8.30am** What is the time 2 hours later?	

© Network Educational Press Ltd

Mathematical understanding is improved when pupils are encouraged to use spoken and written language appropriate to their development, in order to gain meaning from their mathematical experiences.

Put up examples of pupils' own questions on display. Invite groups to look at and perhaps work on other groups' suggestions.

© Network Educational Press Ltd

Fraction familiarity

UNIT 6

Main focus

Developing a feel for relative values of fractions by making physical models

Content

Comparison of fractions of a whole, using $\frac{1}{2}$s and $\frac{1}{3}$s as a basis

Notes for teachers

It is important that pupils make and manipulate physical models of fractions in order to understand their relative values.

Some pupils might experience difficulty in folding and cutting accurately and teachers may want to cut out the strips in advance.

Teachers should encourage pupils to talk about their fraction arrangements to ensure that they begin to match their language with fraction notation.

If pupils find some of the questions difficult, teachers should help by asking questions such as: 'How many eighths in a quarter?'

It is useful to have class discussions at appropriate stages throughout the activity.

It might help to have sets of fractions kits on card for ease of handling.

Learning outcomes

The pupils are able to:

- see and understand relative values of fractions by making physical representations;
- demonstrate equivalence such as $\frac{2}{2} = \frac{3}{3} = 1, \frac{3}{4} = \frac{6}{8}, \frac{3}{12} = \frac{1}{4}$, using models and charts.

Evaluation

Could the pupils:

- fold the strips reasonably accurately?
- label appropriately?
- begin to make connections between different parts of 1 whole?
- arrange fractions in order of size using the strips?
- read and translate fraction charts?

Further activity

Use the fractions kit to help pupils solve questions involving fractions from the school's scheme of work or other resources/materials.

Resources

Pupil task sheets, two A4 sheets of paper per pupil, scissors, envelopes/ boxes, ruler

- *Fold-a-Fraction* sets of three cards can be very helpful. Available from: Craftpack Educational Supplies, 19 Brook Avenue, Warsash, Southampton SO3 9HP Tel. 01489 557676. Fax 01489 572198.
- *Overhead Fraction Strips* are a very useful resource for a plenary session. Available from: Taskmasters Ltd., Morris Road, Leicester, LE2 6BR Tel. 0116 270 4286. Fax 0116 270 6992

© Network Educational Press Ltd

Making and using a fractions kit

You will need:

- 2 A4 sheets of paper
- Scissors
- 1 envelope

- Fold 1 sheet at a time lengthways to get 4 equal strips. You will need 8 strips.

- Take 1 strip and label it 1 whole.

- Take another strip and fold it into half as shown and label each part ½.

- Take another strip and fold it carefully in half twice and label each part ¼.

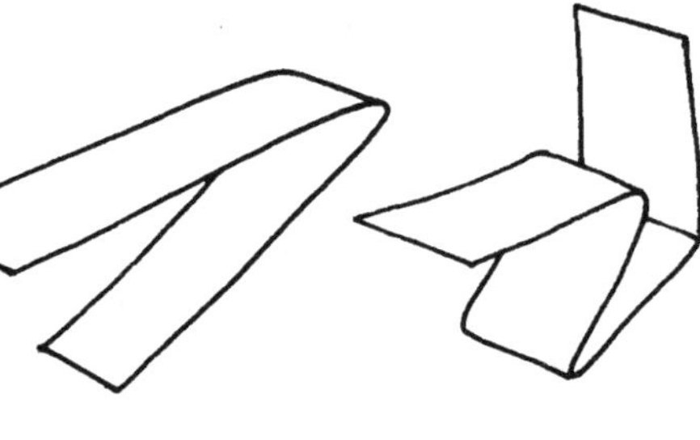

- Take another strip and this time fold it in half 3 times. Be careful to fold it accurately. Label each part ⅛.

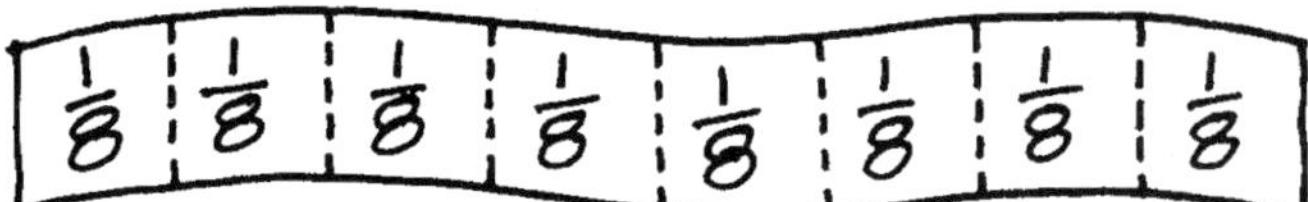

- Continue with the fifth strip and fold very carefully four times and label each part 1/16.

© Network Educational Press Ltd

Making and using a fractions kit

- **Open and line up all the strips.**
  Use your strips to help you complete the missing numbers:

<table>
<tr><td colspan="16">one whole</td></tr>
<tr><td colspan="8">1/2</td><td colspan="8"></td></tr>
<tr><td colspan="4"></td><td colspan="4"></td><td colspan="4">1/4</td><td colspan="4"></td></tr>
<tr><td colspan="2"></td><td colspan="2"></td><td colspan="2"></td><td colspan="2"></td><td colspan="2"></td><td colspan="2"></td><td colspan="2">1/8</td><td colspan="2"></td></tr>
<tr><td></td><td></td><td></td><td></td><td>1/16</td><td></td><td></td><td></td><td></td><td></td><td></td><td></td><td></td><td></td><td></td><td></td></tr>
</table>

A $1 = \frac{2}{2} = \frac{\dots}{4} = \frac{\dots}{8} = \frac{\dots}{16}$

B $\frac{3}{4} = \frac{\dots}{8} = \frac{\dots}{16}$

C $\frac{3}{8} = \frac{\dots}{16}$

D $\frac{4}{16} = \frac{\dots}{8} = \frac{\dots}{4}$

E $\frac{7}{8} = \frac{\dots}{16}$

Check your answers before cutting up all the strips into fractional parts to make your **fractions kit**.

Put these in a box or an envelope.

Now take the next 3 strips.

- Fold 1 strip into 3 equal sections. This can be done by measuring or folding! (Discuss this and use the best method.) Label each part $\frac{1}{3}$.

- Take the next strip and make thirds, as above. Fold each third in half. Label each part $\frac{1}{6}$.

- Take the last strip and make sixths, as above. Fold each sixth in half. Label each of the 12 parts $\frac{1}{12}$.

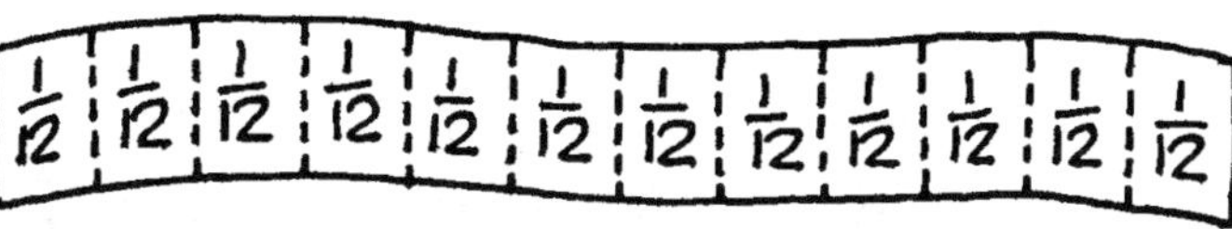

© Network Educational Press Ltd

Making and using a fractions kit

- **Open and line up all the strips. Use your strips to help you complete the missing numbers.**

<table>
<tr><td colspan="4">$\frac{1}{3}$</td><td colspan="4"></td><td colspan="4"></td></tr>
<tr><td colspan="2"></td><td colspan="2">$\frac{1}{6}$</td><td colspan="2"></td><td colspan="2"></td><td colspan="2"></td><td colspan="2"></td></tr>
<tr><td></td><td></td><td></td><td>$\frac{1}{12}$</td><td></td><td></td><td></td><td></td><td></td><td></td><td></td><td></td></tr>
</table>

A $\frac{3}{4} = \frac{\dots\dots}{6} = \frac{\dots\dots}{3}$

B $1 = \frac{\dots\dots}{6} = \frac{\dots\dots}{12} = \frac{3}{\dots\dots}$

C $\frac{3}{4} = \frac{10}{\dots\dots}$

D $\frac{3}{4} = \frac{2}{\dots\dots} = \frac{\dots\dots}{6}$

E $\frac{3}{4} = \frac{6}{\dots\dots} = \frac{\dots\dots}{6}$

Check your answers before cutting all the strips into fractional parts to add to your **fractions kit**.

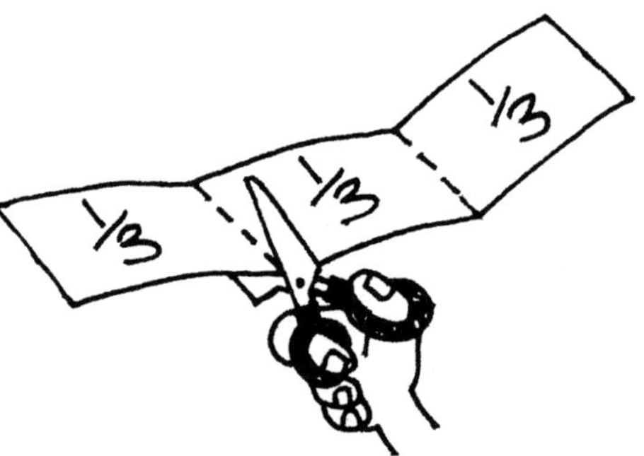

Keep your kit in an envelope or a box and write your name on it.

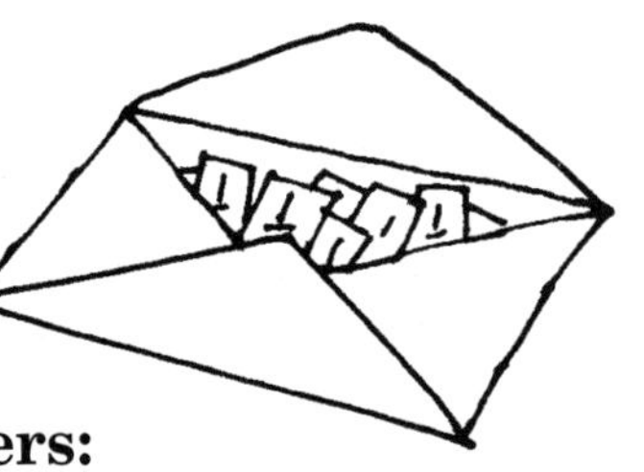

Use your kit to fill in the missing numbers:

A $\frac{1}{4} + \frac{1}{8} = \frac{\dots\dots}{16}$

B $\frac{3}{4} + \frac{3}{8} = \dots\dots$

C $\frac{1}{3} + \frac{1}{6} = \frac{\dots\dots}{6}$

D $\frac{1}{3} + \frac{5}{12} = \dots\dots$

E $\frac{6}{12} = \frac{\dots\dots}{2} = \frac{\dots\dots}{16}$

F $\frac{1}{4} + \frac{\dots\dots}{12} = \frac{\dots\dots}{16}$

G $\frac{1}{2} + \frac{3}{12} = \dots\dots$

H $\frac{4}{16} + \frac{1}{4} + \frac{3}{12} = \dots\dots$

Make up some of your own questions using your **fractions kit** and ask your friends to solve these.

© Network Educational Press Ltd

Fraction strips

A Look at the strips below. What fraction of the whole strip is shaded? Write your answers in the boxes.

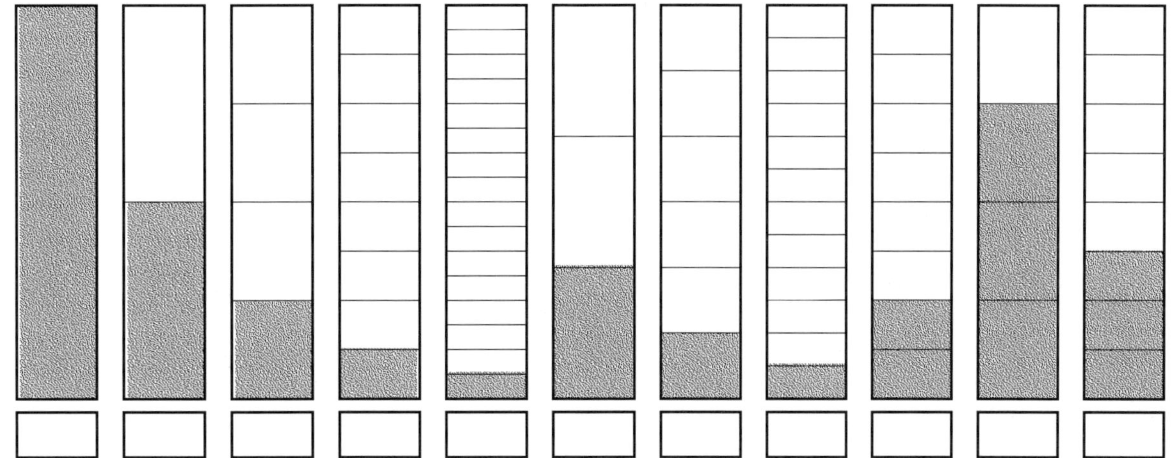

B Now look at these. Can you find out how much is shaded? Write your answers in the boxes.

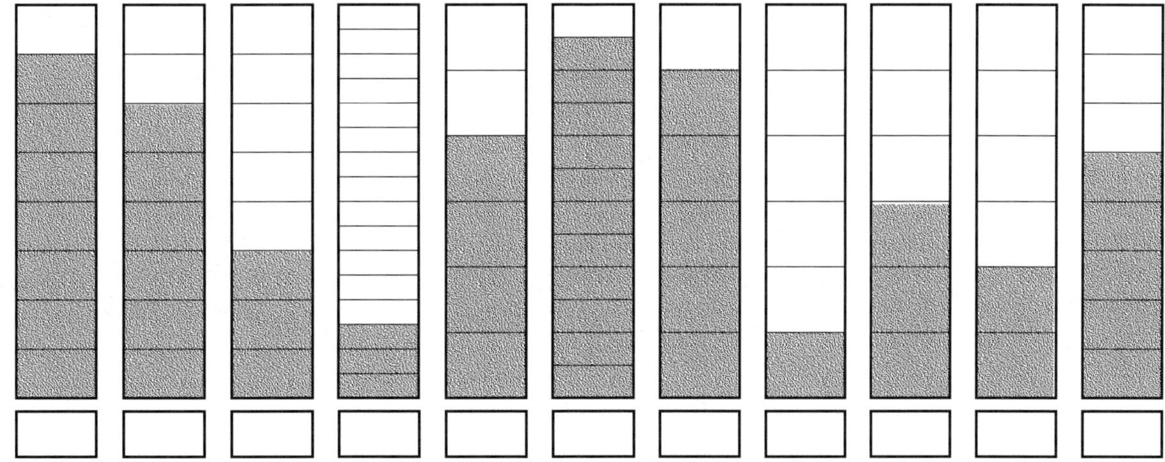

C Write the missing numbers. Use your charts to help you with these:

1 $\frac{1}{2} = \frac{\dots}{6} = \frac{\dots}{12} = \frac{\dots}{10}$

2 $\frac{3}{4} = \frac{\dots}{12} = \frac{\dots}{16}$

3 $\frac{5}{6} = \frac{3}{\dots}$

4 $\frac{1}{3} = \frac{\dots}{6} = \frac{\dots}{9} = \frac{4}{12}$

D Use your charts to help you with these:

5 $\frac{1}{2} + \frac{1}{4} = \dots$

6 $\frac{2}{5} + \frac{3}{10} = \dots$

7 $\frac{1}{3} + \frac{1}{6} = \dots$

8 $\frac{3}{8} + \frac{3}{16} = \dots$

Keep this chart with you to help you with other work on fractions.

© Network Educational Press Ltd

Mathematical understanding is improved when pupils are encouraged to describe and record relationships, as well as to discover and create patterns.

Think how you might 'twist' tasks and questions described in textbooks, worksheets or test papers, so that pupils can become more involved in making decisions, describing patterns and relationships, and testing conjectures.

© Network Educational Press Ltd

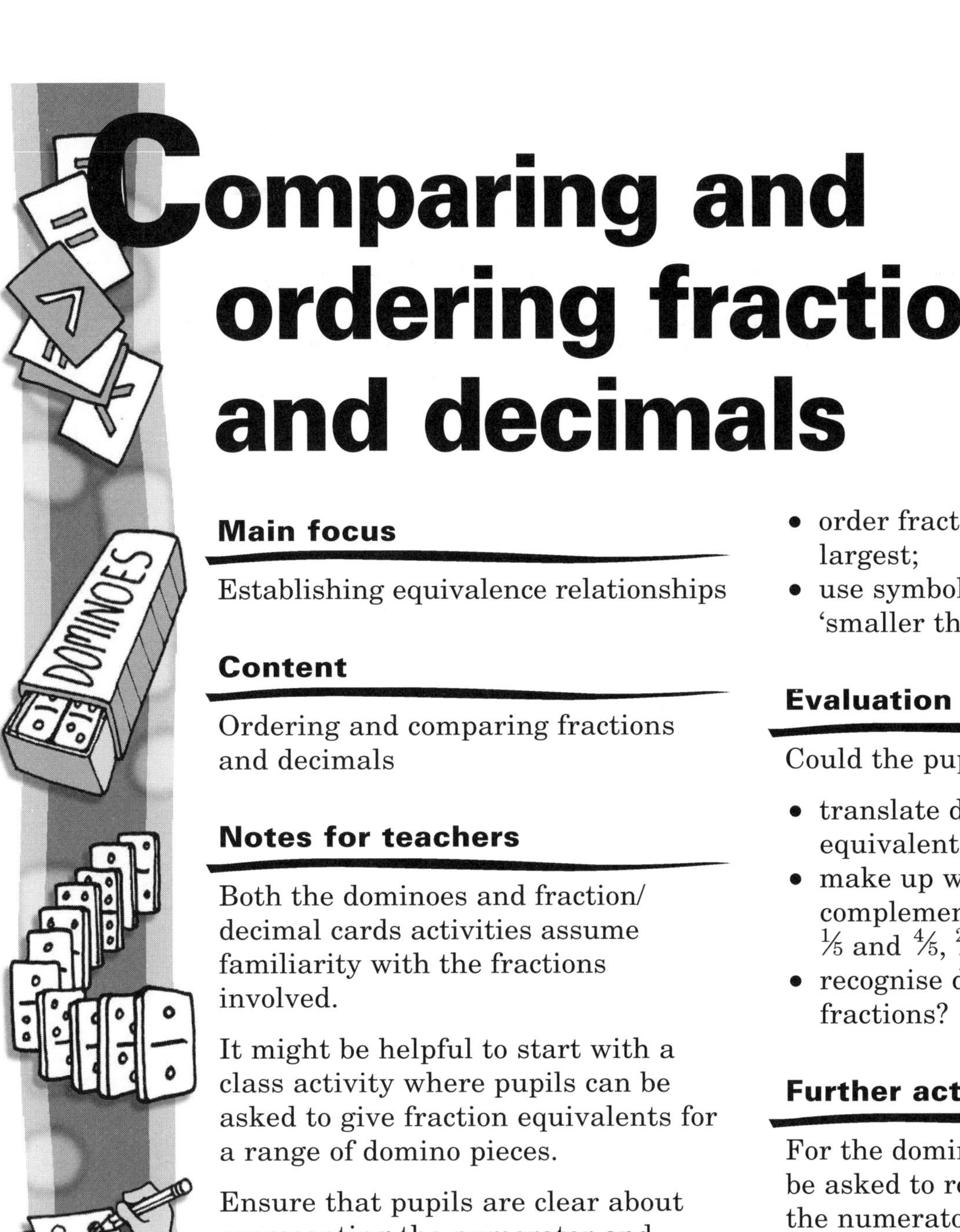

Comparing and ordering fractions and decimals

Main focus

Establishing equivalence relationships

Content

Ordering and comparing fractions and decimals

Notes for teachers

Both the dominoes and fraction/decimal cards activities assume familiarity with the fractions involved.

It might be helpful to start with a class activity where pupils can be asked to give fraction equivalents for a range of domino pieces.

Ensure that pupils are clear about representing the numerator and denominator of the dominoes consistently, i.e. colouring the dots to distinguish between them.

Encourage the pupils to check their answers and record their work.

Pupils can either cut out the required dominoes from the sheet or use real dominoes.

Learning outcomes

The pupils are able to:

- translate information from 'dot' forms to numbers;
- use language associated with fractions and decimals;
- order fractions from smallest to largest;
- use symbols for 'greater than' and 'smaller than' appropriately.

Evaluation

Could the pupils:

- translate dot patterns into fraction equivalents?
- make up whole numbers by adding complementary fractions such as $\frac{1}{5}$ and $\frac{4}{5}$, $\frac{2}{3}$ and $\frac{2}{6}$?
- recognise decimal equivalent of fractions?

Further activity

For the dominoes, able pupils could be asked to reverse the position of the numerator and denominator and arrange them in 3 rows to find new totals. For example, can they make a total of 10 for each row?

The class could discuss the following question: 'What fraction are the dots on the top of the ones on the bottom?'

For the fraction/decimal cards, blank cards have been included so that the range of fractions/decimals can be extended.

Resources

Domino cards, fraction/decimal cards, paper for recording, copies of pupil task sheets, a few sets of dominoes (optional)

© Network Educational Press Ltd

From dominoes to fractions

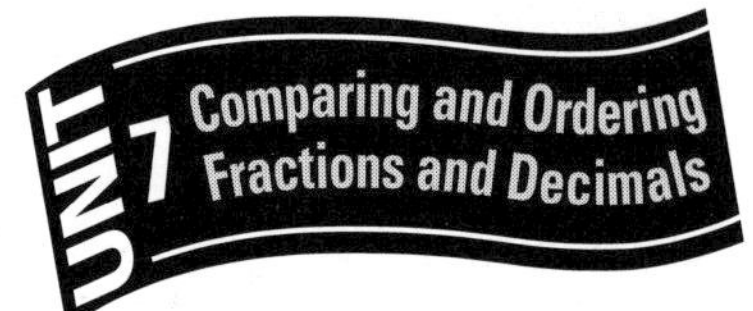

You will need to use these dominoes. Shade the top spots in one colour and the bottom spots in a different colour.

Write down all the dominoes as fractions.

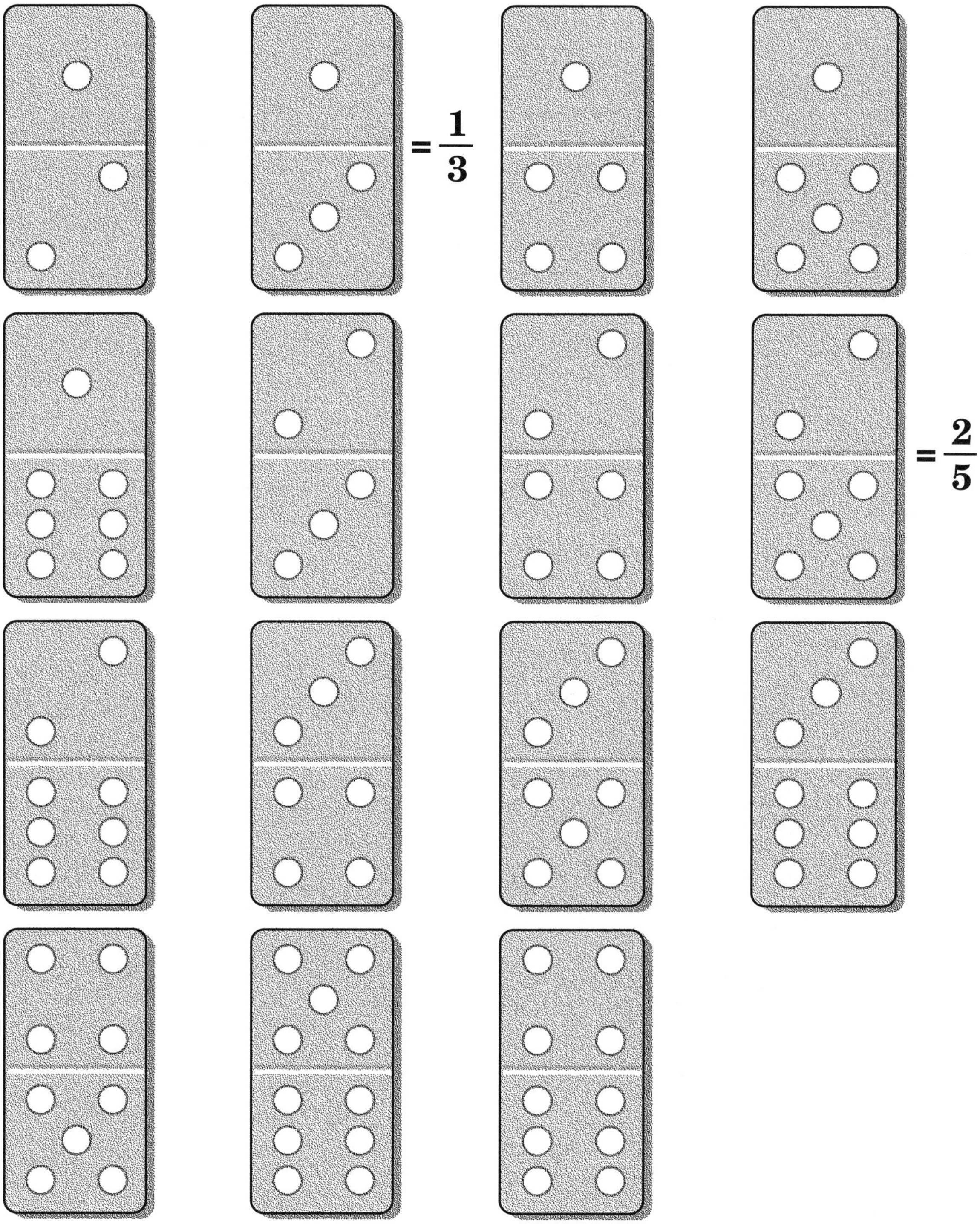

$= \frac{1}{3}$

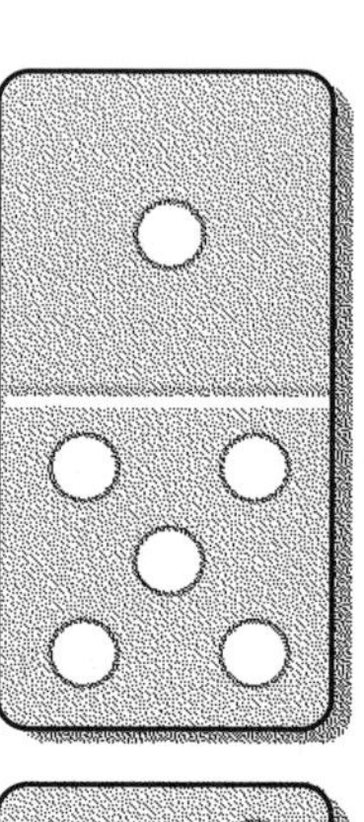

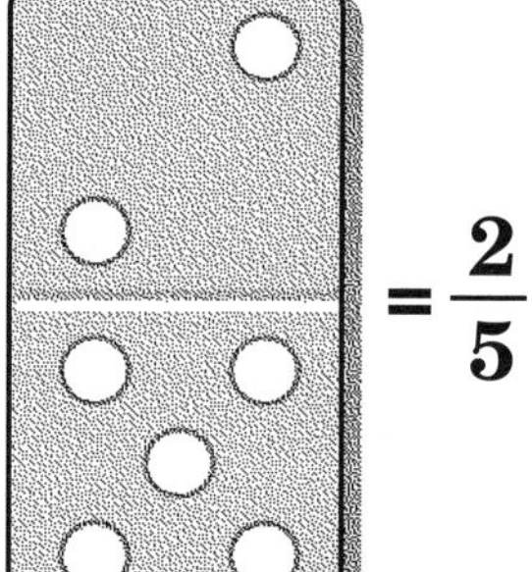

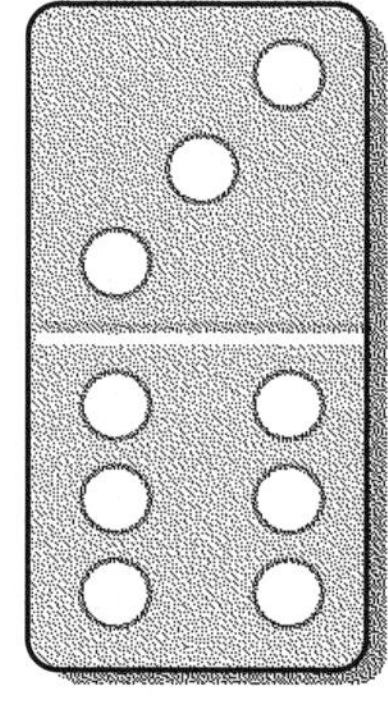

© Network Educational Press Ltd

From dominoes to fractions

Some of the dominoes have been arranged for you.

Use the dominoes left over so that each row adds up to 2½.
(Use your fraction chart to help you.)

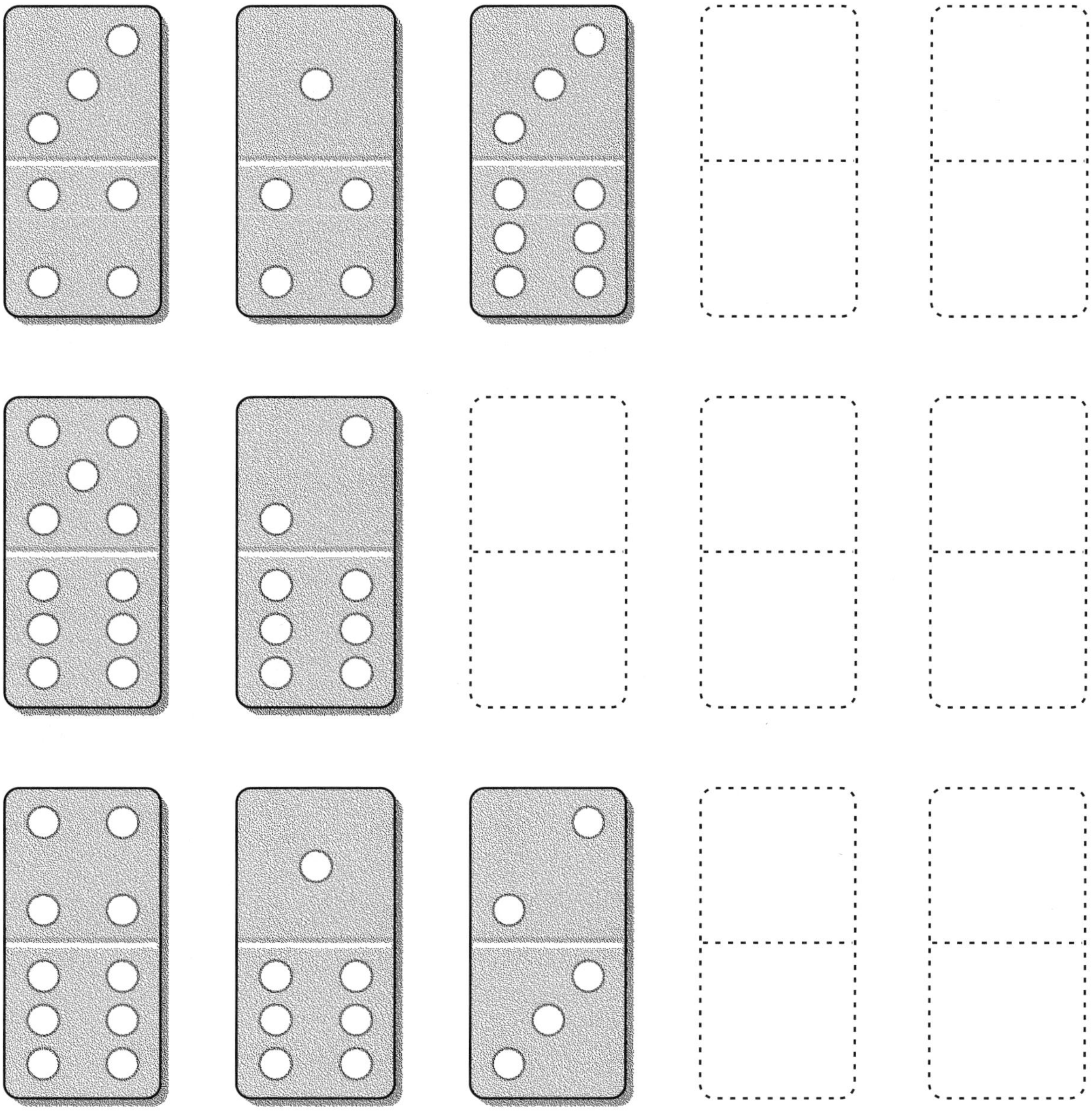

Now choose your own dominoes to find different totals for each row.
Keep a record of your working.

© Network Educational Press Ltd

Dominoes chart

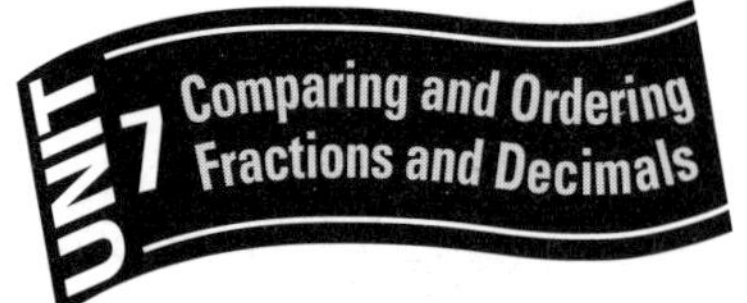

© Network Educational Press Ltd

Ordering fractions and decimals

UNIT 7 Comparing and Ordering Fractions and Decimals

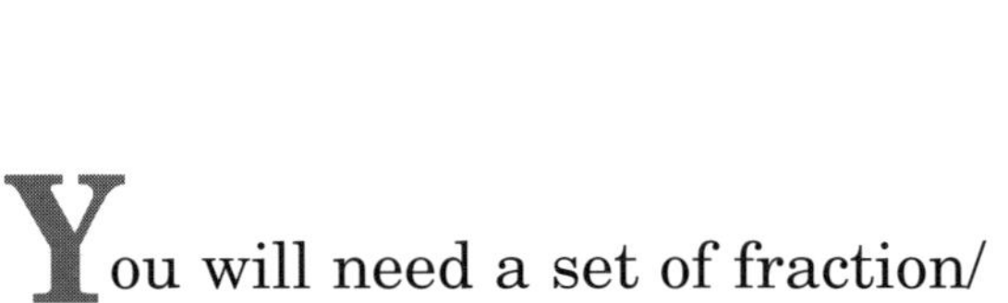

You will need a set of fraction/decimal cards. You can play this in pairs or on your own.

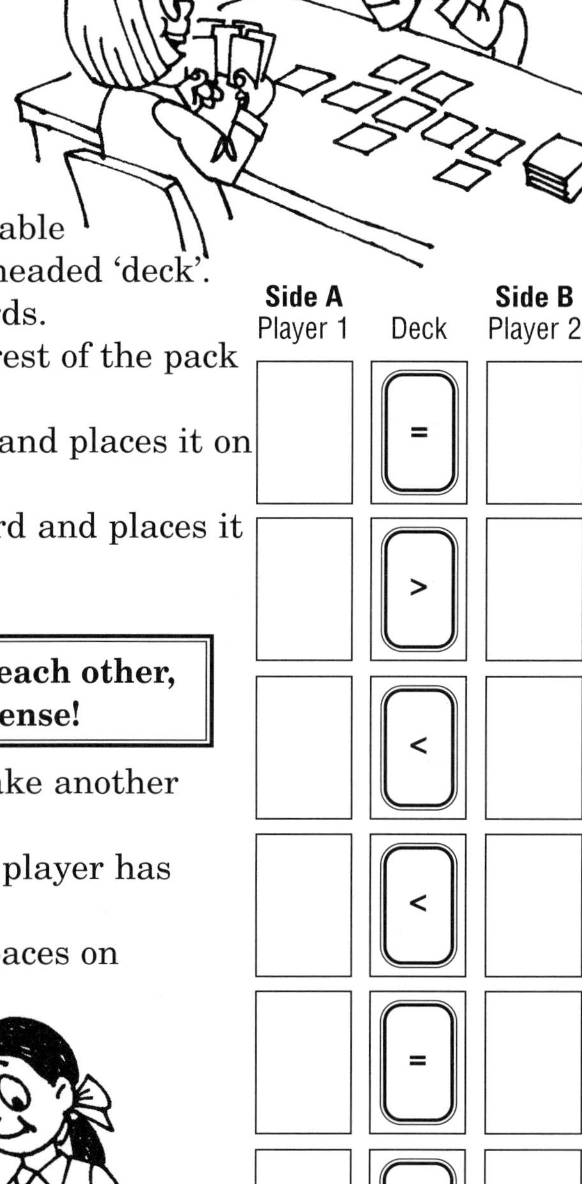

A game for two players

1. Place the symbol cards on the table as shown below in the column headed 'deck'.
2. Shuffle the fraction/decimal cards.
3. Deal 6 cards each and put the rest of the pack face down on the table.
4. The first player chooses 1 card and places it on Side A.
5. The second player chooses a card and places it anywhere on Side B.

If you place the cards opposite each other, the sentence must make sense!

6. Continue — if you cannot go, take another card from the pack.
7. If you still cannot go, the other player has a turn.
8. The first player to fill all the spaces on Side A or Side B wins.

Side A Player 1	Deck	**Side B** Player 2
	=	
	>	
	<	
	<	
	=	
	>	

A game for one player

1. Shuffle the cards.
2. Place the symbol cards on the table.
3. Draw cards from the pack, 1 by 1, and place them to make sensible sentences.
4. Time yourself and see if you can beat your own record.

© Network Educational Press Ltd

Fraction/decimal cards

$\frac{1}{2}$	0.5	$\frac{1}{4}$	0.25	$<$	$>$
$\frac{3}{4}$	0.75	$\frac{1}{10}$	0.1	$<$	$>$
$\frac{1}{5}$	0.2	$\frac{2}{5}$	0.4	$=$	$=$
$\frac{1}{2}$	0.5	$\frac{9}{10}$	0.9		
$\frac{1}{3}$	$\frac{4}{8}$	$\frac{2}{8}$	$\frac{4}{10}$		

© Network Educational Press Ltd

Estimate and check

Main focus

Improving strategies for estimation, introductory sampling techniques, recording systematically

Content

Choosing appropriate units of length, mass capacity and time

Devising techniques appropriate for checking estimations

Recording and reporting experiments

Notes for teachers

These activities would need to be carried out over an extended period.

It is useful to begin with a discussion on estimation and on sensible units to use. Ask pupils to consider how they could improve on the accuracy of their estimates.

For Estimate and Check Activity 1, ask pupils for ideas on how they could solve the problems, for example arm reaches, pigeon steps, metre rules. Encourage pupils to check their results using another method. After the activity, talk about the best methods and establish a sensible range of answers.

The Estimate and Check Activity 2 is designed so that it would be impossible for pupils to ascertain an exact answer. Discuss choice of approach with pupils and how it could help them to obtain better answers.

It is useful to ask pupils to report back their findings part-way through the investigations. All the pupils could try out the first activity, but for the second it is better for the teacher to assign tasks to particular groups.

Methods of recording should be discussed.

Learning outcomes

The pupils are able to:

- make sensible estimates in realistic contexts;
- improve measuring skills;
- round up or down to give appropriate answers;
- organise and record their work systematically;
- record and write a clear report.

Evaluation

Could the pupils:

- offer reasonable initial estimates?
- contribute effectively to the group task?
- plan and organise their experiments?
- choose an appropriate level of accuracy for the activities?
- communicate their findings in writing?

Further activity

Ask pupils to devise similar problems using other contexts in the school environment and to make a presentation of their findings to the rest of the class.

Resources

Metre rules, weighing scales, litre measure, bucket, stop watch, string, scissors, hoops, calculators, pupil task sheets

© Network Educational Press Ltd

Activity 1

Write down your estimates for the following:

How tall is the tree in or near the school grounds?

How many acorns are there in a kilogram?

Some taps drip all the time. How much water drips from a tap in 15 minutes? An hour? A day? A week? A year?

How many different plants can be enclosed by a hoop?

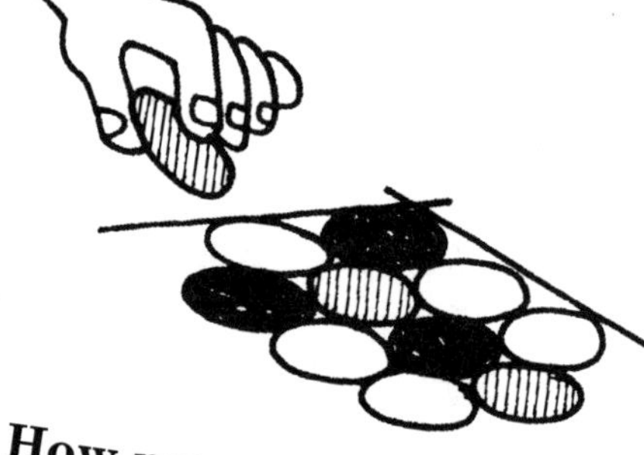

How many counters can be enclosed in a square 30 cm by 30 cm?

Carry out an experiment to check your estimates in some or all cases.

© Network Educational Press Ltd

Activity 2

In your group choose one of the following questions:

How many pupils are there in the school? Could we get every family into the school hall?

How many words are there in all the books in the class library?

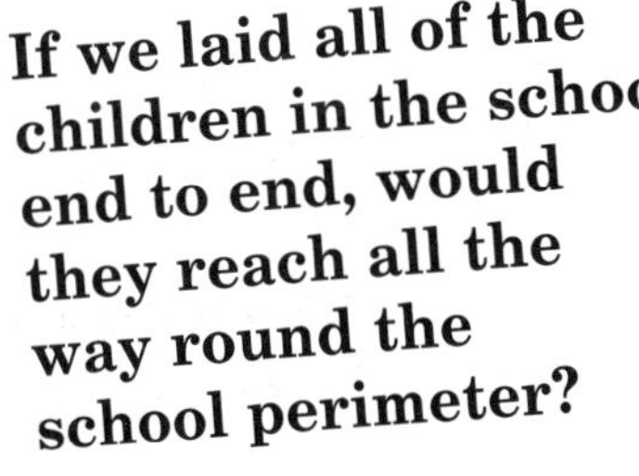

If we laid all of the children in the school end to end, would they reach all the way round the school perimeter?

Which is more likely to be the larger sum — one week's pocket money for all the children in the school, or £200?

Which is heavier — all of the children in the school, or 5 tonnes?

Estimate your answer.
Carry out an experiment to check your estimate. You will need the Estimation Checksheet to help you.

© Network Educational Press Ltd

Estimation checksheet: activity 2

UNIT 8 Estimate and Check

Name ....

Our experiment

We think the answer is about:

....

We came to that conclusion because:

....

....

....

To find a sensible answer we will need to find out:

....

....

....

BE SYSTEMATIC!

Who will we ask?

....

Why have we chosen these people?

....

Who in our group will do what?

....

....

© Network Educational Press Ltd

Estimate checksheet: activity 2

Prepare a recording table.

....

....

....

....

....

....

....

....

....

Look at your results.

....

....

....

....

....

....

....

....

....

Think about:

- **How will you come to an answer?**
- **Was your original idea a good one?**

YOU CANNOT FIND OUT EXACTLY!

Now write a report.

....

....

....

....

....

....

....

....

© Network Educational Press Ltd

Mathematical understanding is improved when skills are sustained through meaningful practice and enjoyable drill.

When you want pupils to practise skills, see if such practice can emerge through pupils' own enquiries, or from problems demanding the use of those skills.

© Network Educational Press Ltd

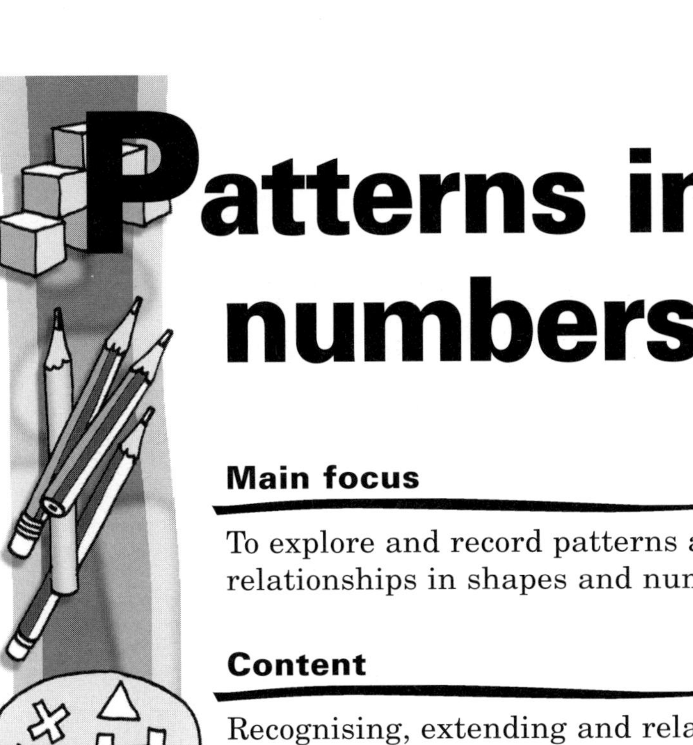

Patterns in numbers

Main focus

To explore and record patterns and relationships in shapes and numbers

Content

Recognising, extending and relating patterns in shapes and numbers

Describing relationships in words

Notes for teachers

These activities are best approached through an initial class discussion.

Discuss suggestions from pupils about the way they see patterns growing.

It is important that pupils meet the same relationships in different contexts and mediums.

Cubes and counters would be useful to model the arrangements of tins and crosses.

The results of these activities provide a good opportunity for pupils to extend mathematical language.

Teachers can help this process by discussing pupils' rules and helping them refine their statements.

Pupils could be asked to display their rules.

Learning outcomes

The pupils are able to:

- recognise and predict patterns;
- explain patterns used;
- identify patterns in number sequences.

Evaluation

Could the pupils:

- spot and extend the pattern and shapes?
- translate the patterns into numbers?
- extend the number sequences?
- explain the relationship in words?
- write the rules in words without ambiguity?

Further activity

Children could be asked to construct their own patterns and write down their own rules. It is useful to ask pupils to discuss their patterns with others and modify their work if necessary.

Resources

Pupil task sheets, square dotted paper

© Network Educational Press Ltd

Tower of tins

A supermarket assistant was asked to make a display of baked bean tins. The display has to be 10 tins high.

How many tins are needed altogether?

Can you find out how many tins will be on the bottom row?

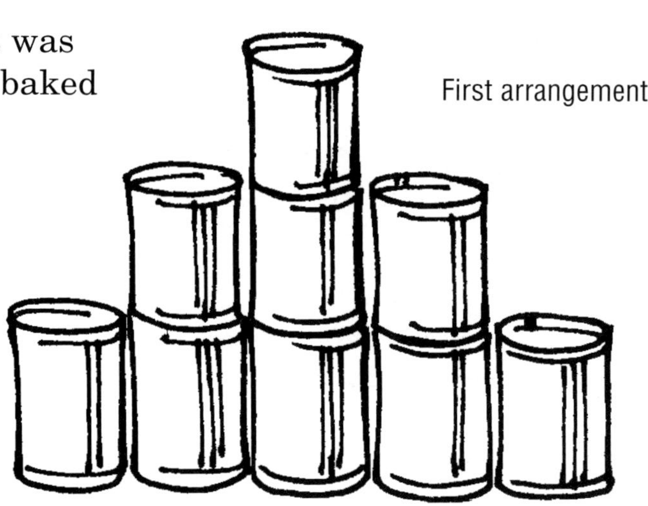

First arrangement

Number of tins high	Number along the bottom	Number altogether
1	1	1
2	3	4
3		
4		
5		
6		
7		
8		
9		
10		

Now complete this chart for the first arrangement.

Can you spot any patterns?

Write down what you notice.

....

....

....

....

....

Can you predict how many tins would be needed for the bottom row of the 15th model?

....

What about the 20th model?

....

© Network Educational Press Ltd

Tower of tins

If the display was built like this, how many tins would be needed this time?

How many tins will be on the bottom row?

Now complete this chart for the second arrangement.

Can you spot any patterns?

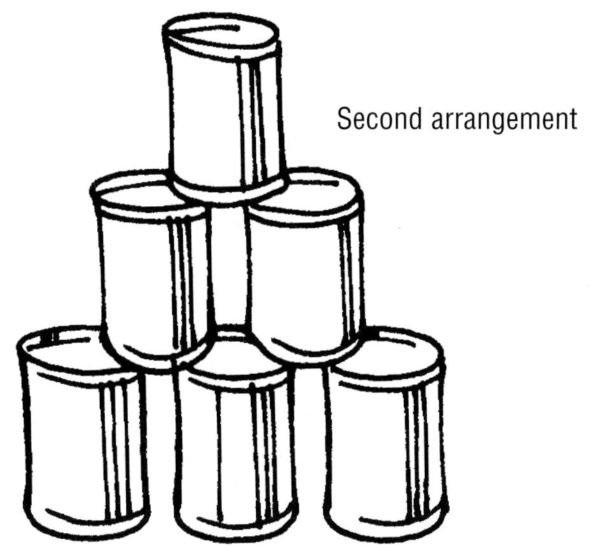

Second arrangement

Number of tins high	Number along the bottom	Number altogether
1	1	1
2	2	3
3		
4		
5		
6		
7		
8		
9		
10		

Write down what you notice.

....

....

....

....

....

Can you predict how many tins would be needed for the bottom row of the 15th model?

....

What about the 20th model?

....

© Network Educational Press Ltd

Describe my growth

Look at these patterns of crosses.

A

		×
	×	×
×	× ×	× × ×

Can you guess what the next 2 patterns would be?
Copy the pattern on dotted paper and draw your 2 patterns.

Now try these.

B

×	× ×	× × ×

C

		× × ×
	× ×	× × ×
×	× ×	× × ×

D

		×
	×	× ×
×	× ×	× × ×

E

		×
	×	×
×	× × ×	× × × × ×
	×	×
		×

© Network Educational Press Ltd

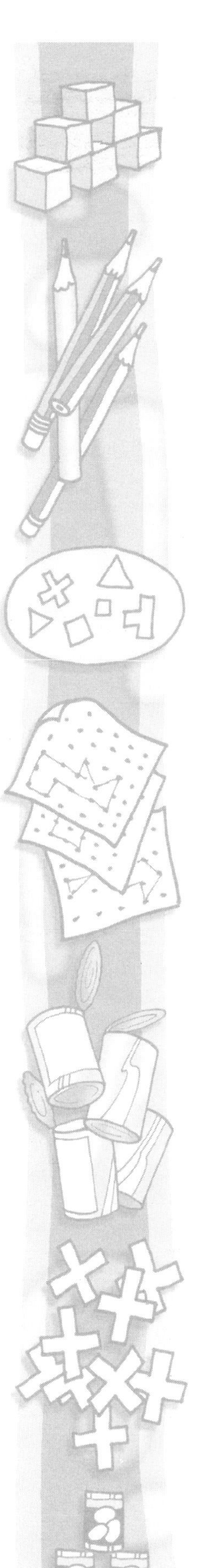

Describe my growth

Look at your patterns again. Record the number of crosses in each pattern in the table.

Can you guess 2 more numbers for each pattern without drawing?

Record these and write down your rule.

	Stage 1	Stage 2	Stage 3	Stage 4	Stage 5	My rule
A	1	3	5			
B						
C						
D						
E						

Make up 3 of your own patterns on the dotted paper and record your numbers and rules on the table.

© Network Educational Press Ltd

Dot to dot

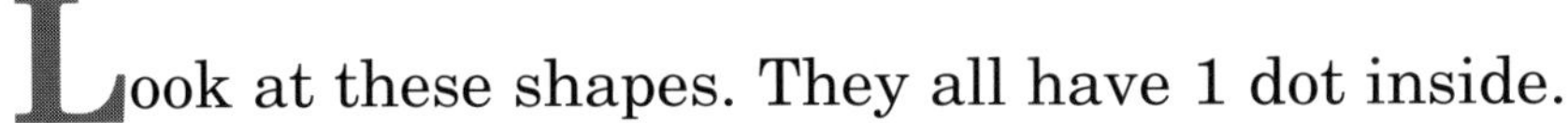
Look at these shapes. They all have 1 dot inside.

How many dots are on the outside (perimeter)?

What is the area?

Shapes with 1 dot inside

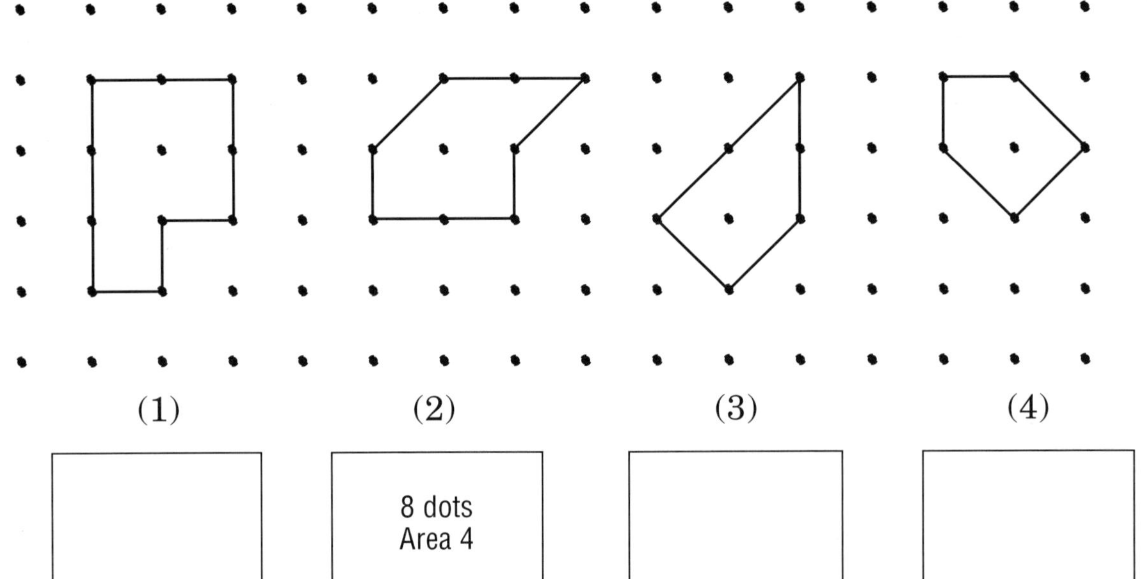

Find 5 more shapes which enclose 1 dot.

Record your results. You will need dotted paper for this. What do you notice?

Try shapes with 2 dots inside them. Can you find any rules or patterns about dots and areas?

Try other numbers of dots inside the enclosures. Is there a pattern?

© Network Educational Press Ltd

© Network Educational Press Ltd

Mathematical understanding is improved when imaginitive use is made of a wide variety of resources.

Encourage pupils to find methods and rules for themselves. Involve them in comparing the methods to agree on the most efficient.

© Network Educational Press Ltd

Reading dials, dates and scales

UNIT 10

Main focus

Interpreting information involving numbers and scales

Content

Reading simple scales on measuring instruments and calculating increase or decrease to the nearest whole number

Reading clocks and calculating time differences

Converting time to the 24-hour clock

Reading dates on packages and making sensible inferences

Notes for teachers

It is important that pupils at this stage can begin to read and interpret the numerical information they encounter.

Teachers may wish to begin the lesson using objects with dials and scales.

The tasks can be used either for diagnostic purposes or for consolidation. A photocopiable sheet of unmarked scales is included. Teachers can use these to set their own practice questions.

In order to encourage mental fluency, teachers could conduct a class lesson by using an overhead transparency or a chart.

Pupils could be invited to invent their own questions using blank scales.

For 'How long to go', teachers should ensure that pupils have understood the difference between 'use by' and 'best before'. Real packages provide greater motivation.

Learning outcomes

The pupils are able to:

- read and interpret information presented in a variety of ways;
- mentally work out the changes illustrated.

Evaluation

Could the pupils:

- read the scales and numbers correctly?
- offer explanations, orally and in writing?
- work out the answers accurately?

Further activity

The unmarked scales sheet could be given to pupils to invent their own questions. This will enable teachers to ascertain if pupils can appreciate the range of sensible data for a given context.

Resources

Pupil task sheets

© Network Educational Press Ltd

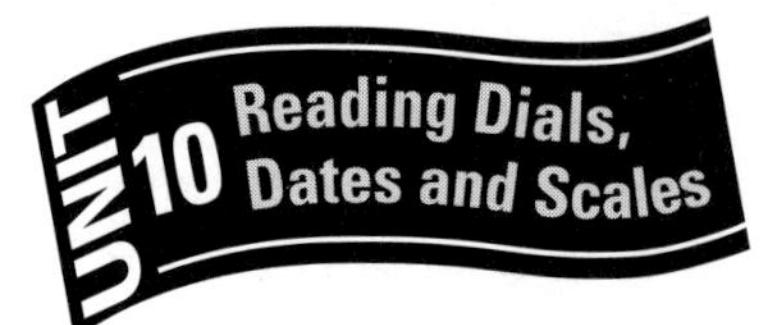

Reading dials and scales

Look at the following series of two pictures.

Write down what has changed and by how much.

12:15

18:20

00430

00770

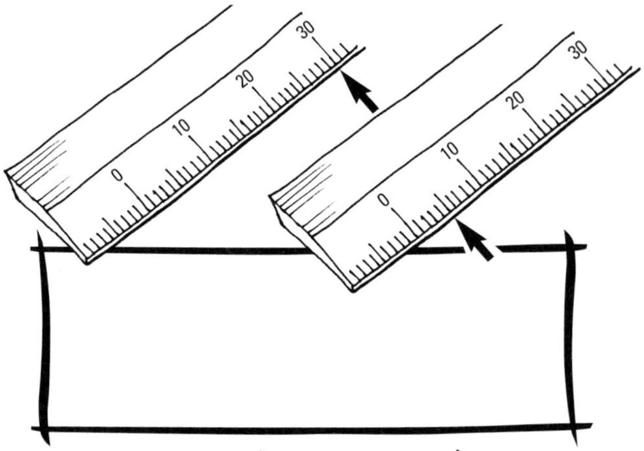

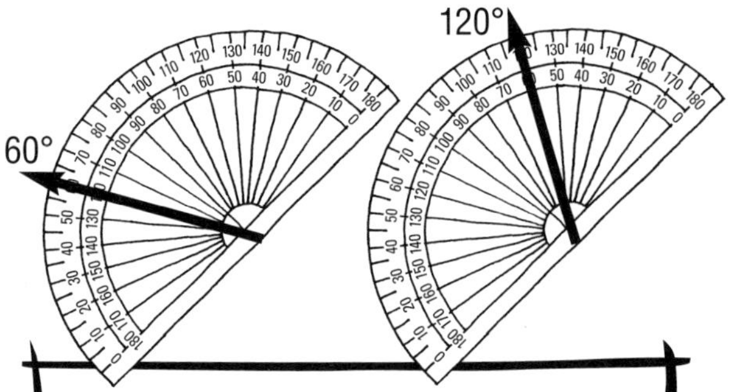

120°

60°

© Network Educational Press Ltd

Reading dials and scales

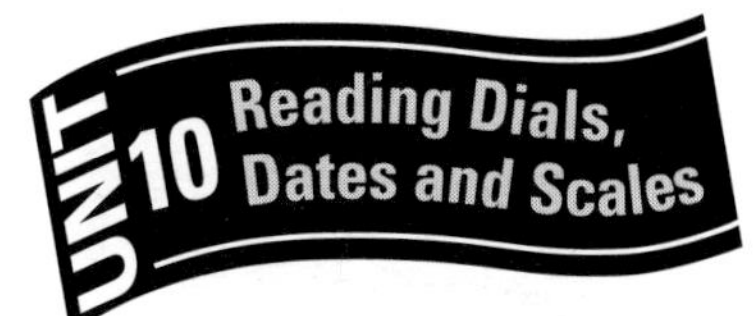

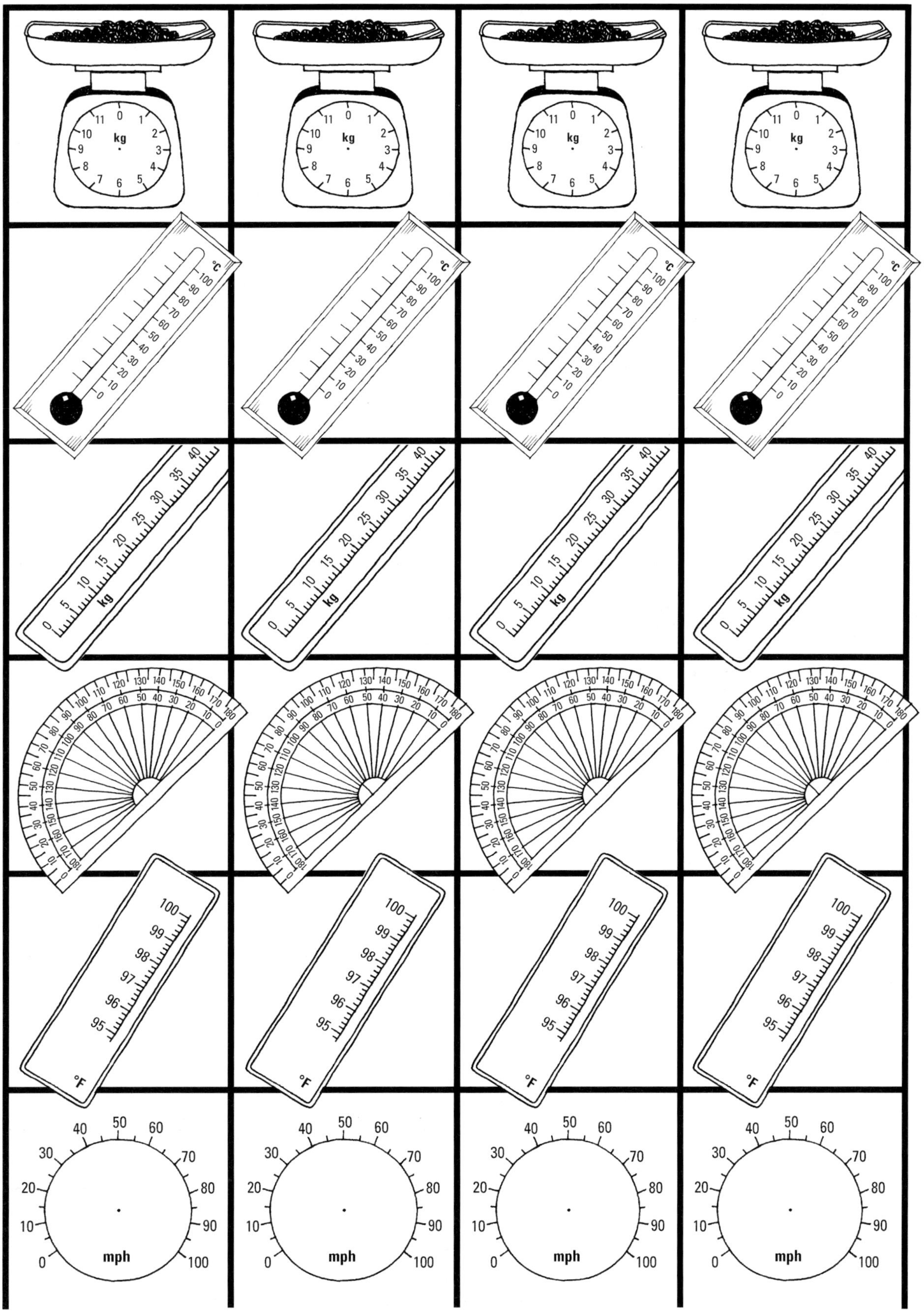

East African time

Kenya and Uganda are in East Africa and lie directly across the equator. The sun rises at about 7.00am every day of the year.

The people of East Africa start their day at 7.00am and, therefore, think of it as the first hour of the day. So although their clock reads 7.00am, people automatically translate this mentally to 1.00am when they tell the time.

Similarly the evening begins at 6.00pm, making 7.00pm the first hour of the evening which is translated into 1.00pm.

This is a traditional way of thinking about time and not used officially.

What time would people in East Africa *say* this was?

....

If you are told that someone goes to bed at 2 o'clock in the evening, don't be surprised! It means 2 hours after the evening begins, in other words 8.00pm.

© Network Educational Press Ltd

East African time

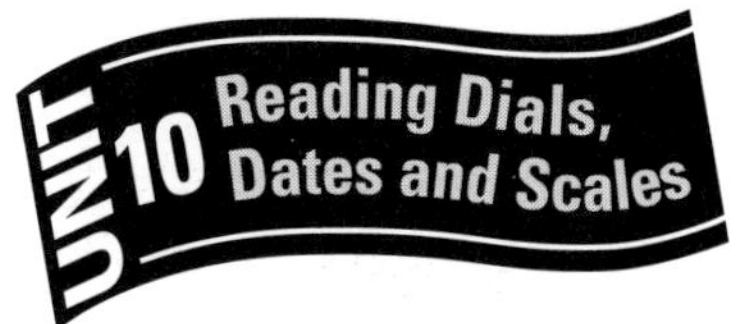

Now see how quickly you can convert Mary's day to the East African way of telling the time. The pictures are in no particular order.

© Network Educational Press Ltd

East African time

East Africa is 2 hours ahead of British Summer Time (BST).

On the 24-hour clock line, mark Mary's day in BST and her actual time in East Africa. Times A and E have been marked for you.

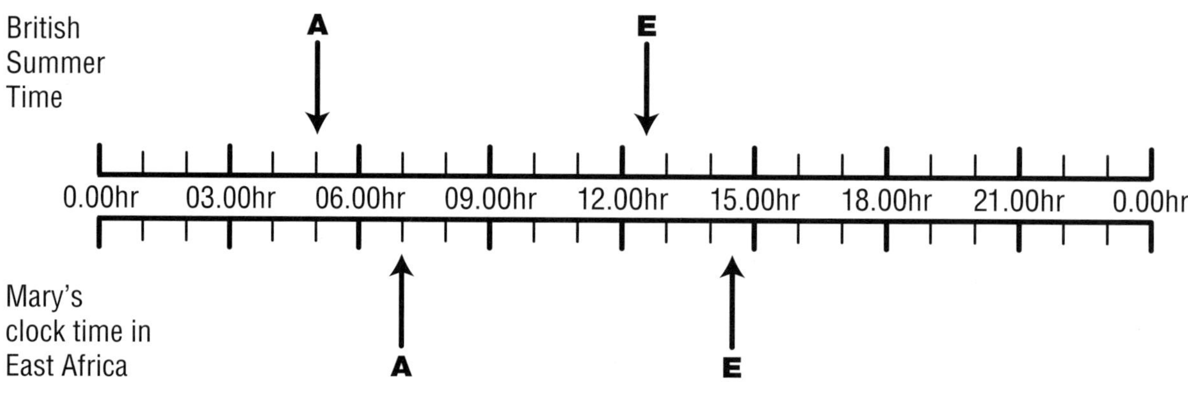

© Network Educational Press Ltd

How long to go?

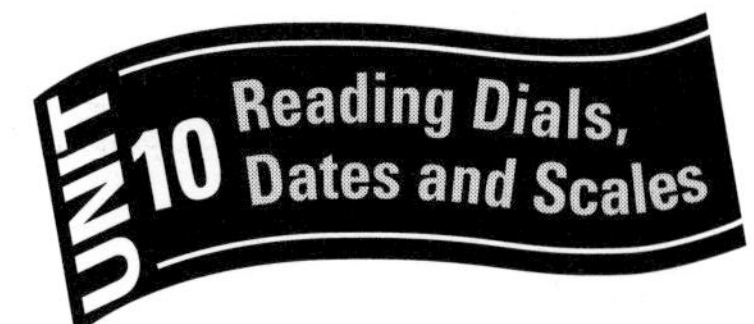

Fill in the spaces

	Date bought	Consume within
Use by 11 January	7 January	.... days
Use by 10 April	29 March	.... days
Eat on day of purchase	6 September	.... days
Use by 2 November	30 October	.... days
Best before 8 June	5 May	.... days

© Network Educational Press Ltd

How long to go?

Fill in the spaces

	Date bought	Consume within
PORK PIE Use by 2 May	30 April	.... days
BURGERS Use by 8 July	5 July	.... days
Happy Birthday Best before 16 January	11 December	.... days
YOGHURT Use by 13 March	9 March	.... days
SAUSAGES Use by 2 March	27 February	.... days

© Network Educational Press Ltd

Simple probability concepts

Main focus

Extending pupils' intuitive understanding of probability

Content

Informal investigations of simple ideas of probability

Predicting and evaluating outcomes of simple experiments

Notes for teachers

At this stage, pupils would have developed a good intuitive understanding of possible and impossible events. They might, however, have difficulty in differentiating between impossible and unlikely events.

It is assumed that pupils have carried out probability experiments such as tossing a coin or rolling a die and compared actual outcomes against expected (theoretical) outcomes.

The activities are designed to promote discussion on outcomes which are not equally likely as pupils often have a false belief that chances are always 'equal'.

It is important that teachers encourage pupils to refine their language and concepts through discussion and writing.

Pooling of class results can lead to a better illustration of the ideas.

Learning outcomes

The pupils are able to:

- appreciate the notion of probability through experience as well as experiment;
- discuss events and experiments using vocabulary such as certain, probably, likely, uncertain, fair;
- record, interpret and represent information using tables, charts and graphs.

Evaluation

Could the pupils:

- classify events with understanding?
- represent and interpret information gathered?
- use the probability scale sensibly?
- understand and use associated vocabulary?
- make sensible observations from the outcomes of experiments?

Further activity

Depending on pupils' familiarity with fractions, ideas of outcomes related to the probability scale between 0 and 1 can be developed.

Resources

Spinners p.84, dominoes, cm^2 grid paper p.86, pupil task sheets

© Network Educational Press Ltd

Impossible, certain or possible?

Work in pairs or in a group. You will need the 12 cards marked A to L. Cut out the cards and shuffle them. Take it in turns to pick a card. Read the card aloud and discuss which column this card should go in. Put the card in the agreed column.

Now each member of the group should try to make a card of their own for each column.

Impossible	Possible	Certain

Take each card from your columns and write a letter (A to L) on the probability line to show where you think the most sensible position for each card is.

Add your own cards too.

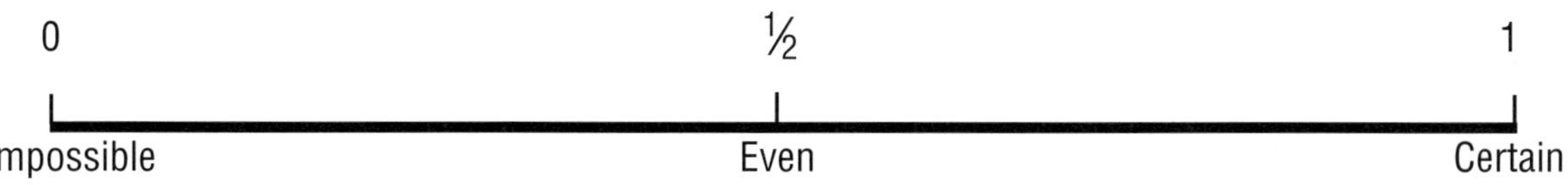

© Network Educational Press Ltd

Impossible, certain or possible?

UNIT 11 Simple Probability Concepts

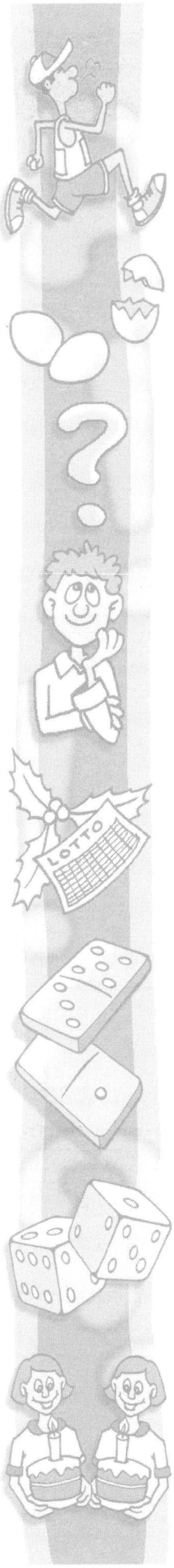

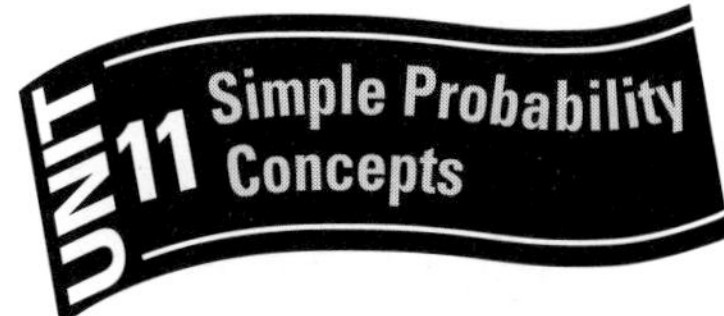

A

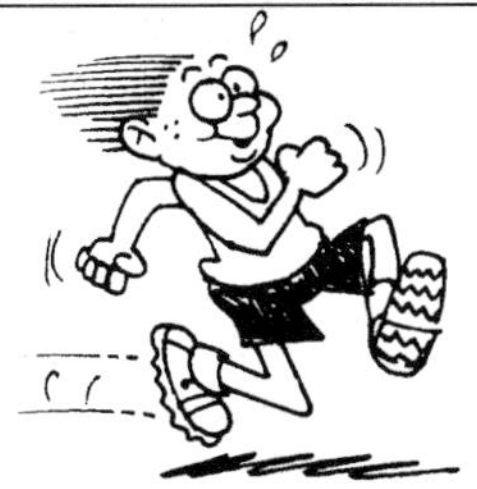

Jack runs a kilometre in 5 seconds

B

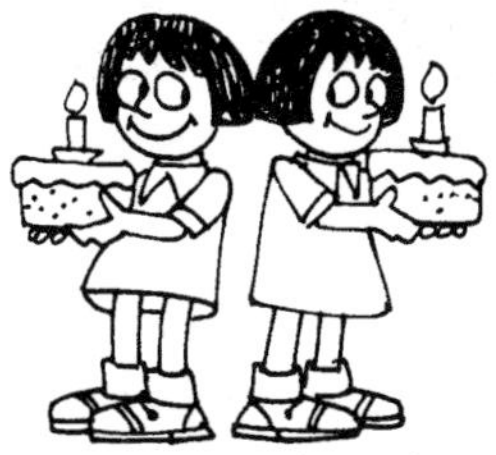

Twins have birthdays on different days

C

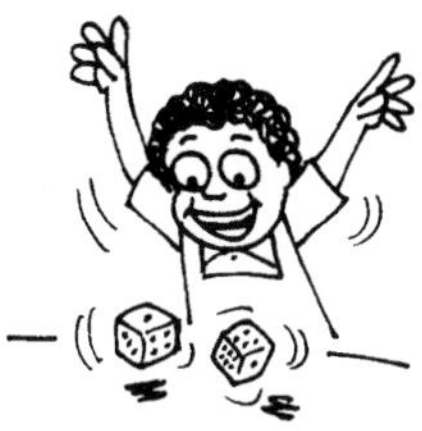

I score 13 when I roll two normal dice

D

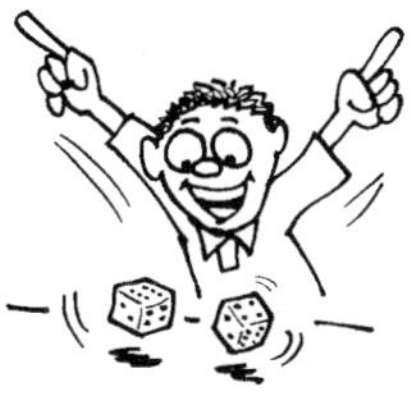

I score a double six when I roll two normal dice

E

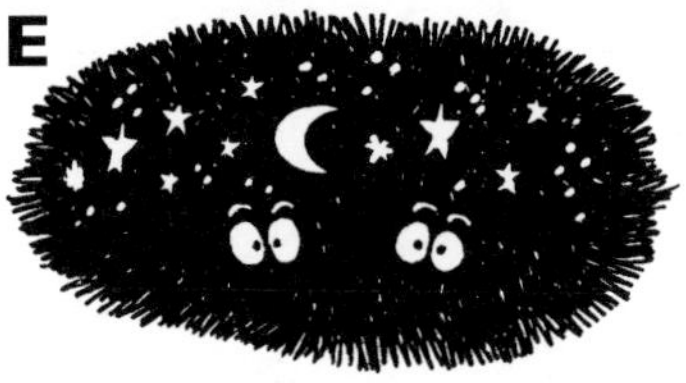

It would get dark in London once every 24 hours

F

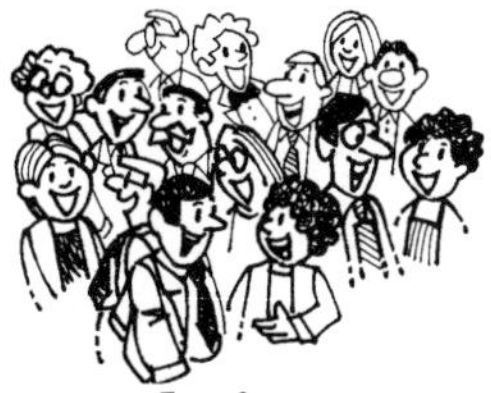

15 people in a room will all have birthdays in different months

G

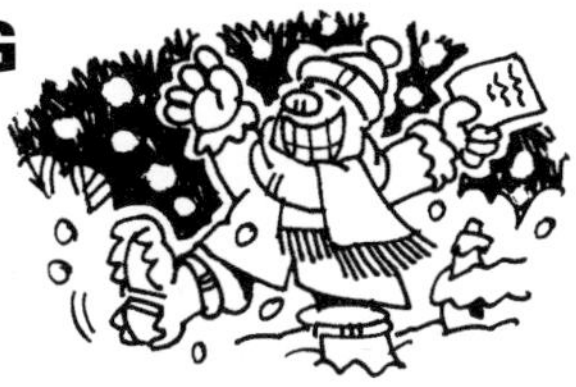

Mr Luck wins the lottery every week in December

H

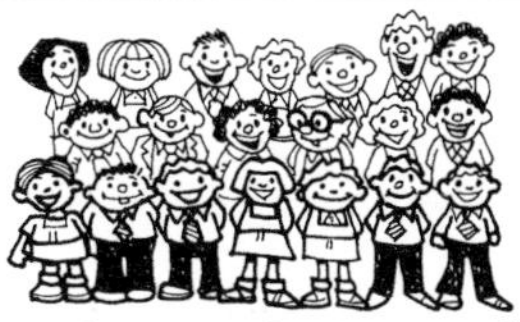

In a class of 20 pupils, at least two pupils have birthdays in the same month

I

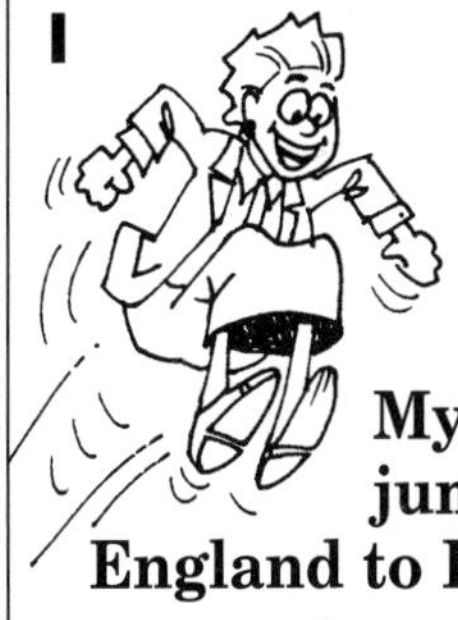

My teacher jumps from England to Ireland

J

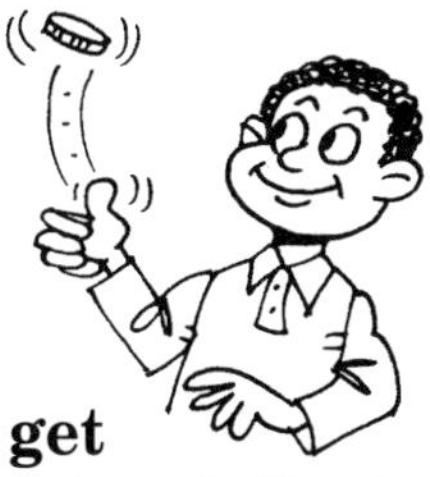

I get a head or tail when I flip a pound coin

K

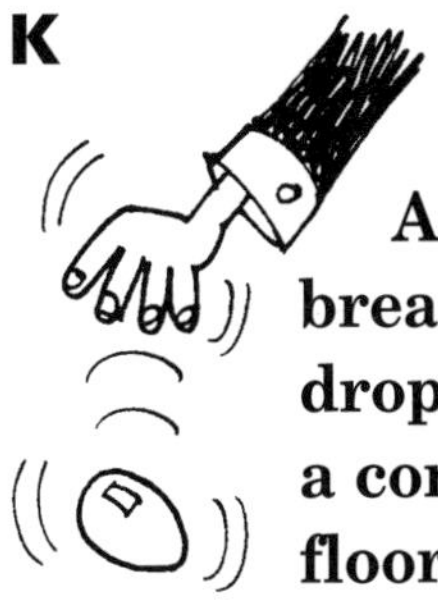

An egg breaks when dropped on a concrete floor

L

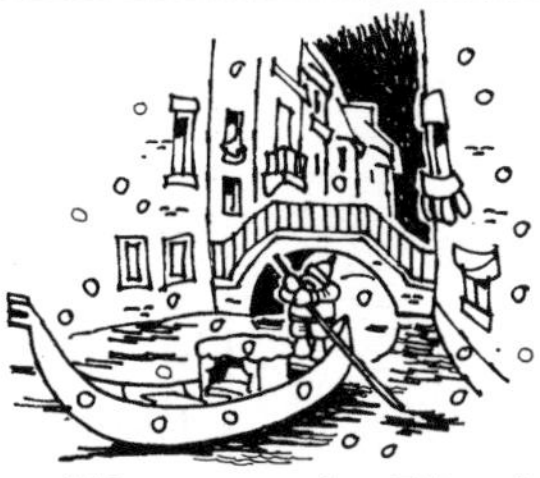

It will snow in Venice every day next year

M

N

O

© Network Educational Press Ltd

Predict and test 1

You will need three spinners.

A

B

C

Before you begin your experiment, write down your guesses and say why.

My Predictions

The spinner most likely to stop on red is

My reason is

The spinner most likely to stop on white is

My reason is

The spinner least likely to stop on yellow is

My reason is

The spinner which has equal chances of stopping on white, blue, yellow or red is

My reason is

© Network Educational Press Ltd

Predict and test 1

Spin your spinners 36 times and record your results.

Spinner A

		Total
Red		
White		
Blue		
Yellow		

Spinner B

		Total
Red		
White		
Blue		
Yellow		

Spinner C

		Total
Red		
White		
Blue		
Yellow		

Show your results on a bar graph.

Look at your predictions and your bar graph. What do you notice?

....

....

....

If you were making up a game, which spinner would you use? Why?

....

....

....

© Network Educational Press Ltd

Predict and test 2

You will need a set of dominoes. Lay out the dominoes face down and shuffle them. Choose one, record the total number of spots and replace it.

Shuffle again and record your total.
Do this 36 times.
Record your results on the chart by putting one cross for each score.

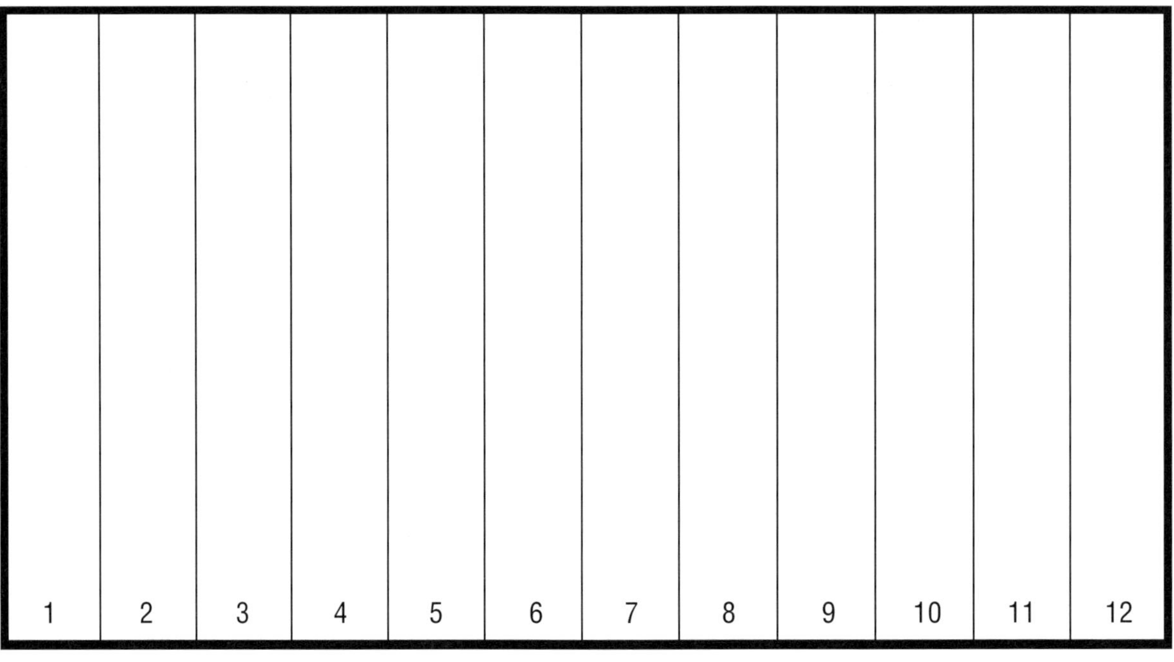

Scores

© Network Educational Press Ltd

Predict and test 2

Now turn your dominoes so that you can see all the spots. Count all the spots on each piece and record the number with a cross in the correct column. You should have 28 crosses.

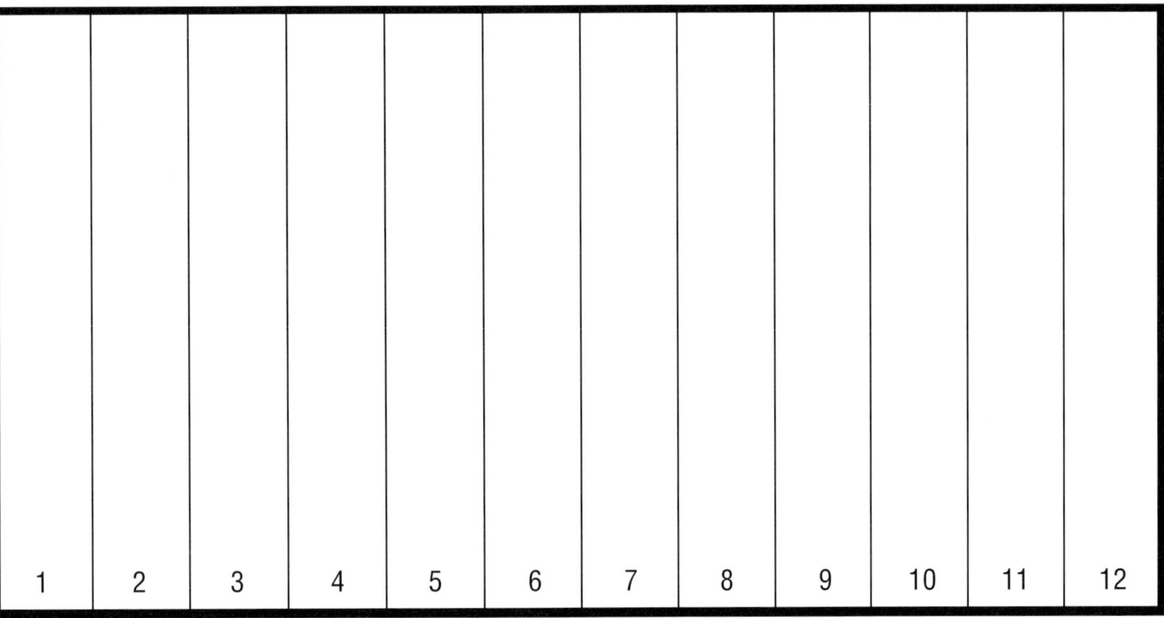

Write down what you notice.

If you were playing a game of shuffling and picking one:

- **which scores do you expect to get most often?** ....
- **which scores do you expect to get least often?** ....

How does your expectation compare with your experiment?

....

....

How can you obtain better results for your experiment?

....

....

....

....

....

© Network Educational Press Ltd

Predict and test spinners

Blue
White
Yellow
Red

Blue
White
Yellow
Red

Blue
Yellow
White
Red

Blue
Yellow
White
Red

Blue
Yellow
Red
White

Blue
Yellow
Red
White

© Network Educational Press Ltd

Domino set

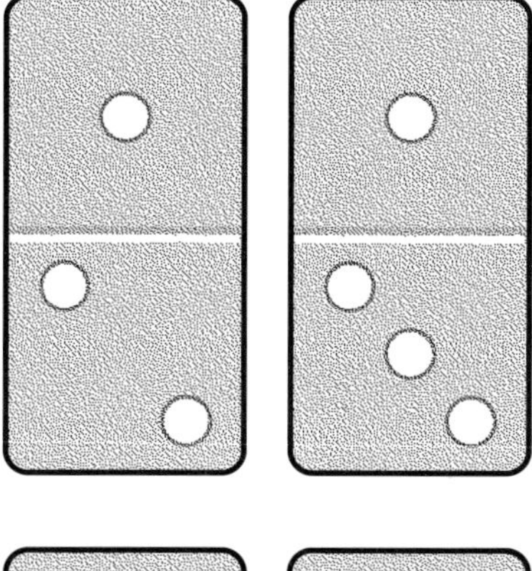
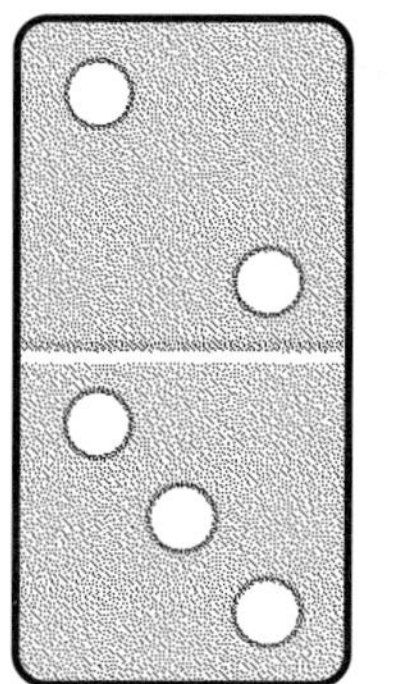
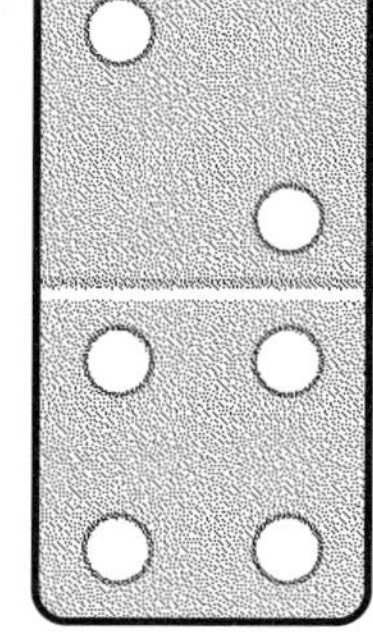
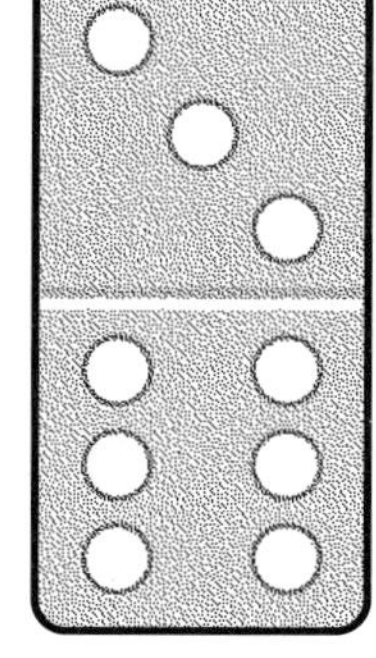
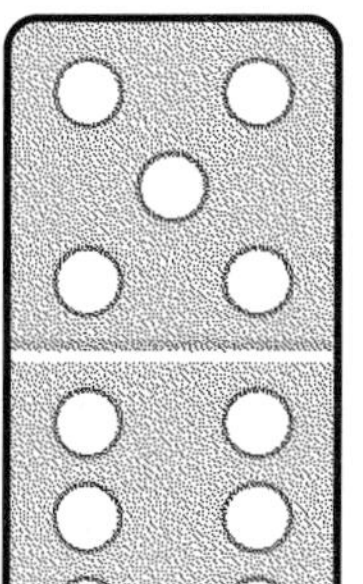
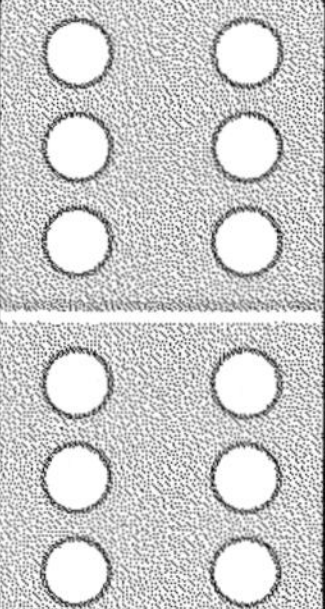

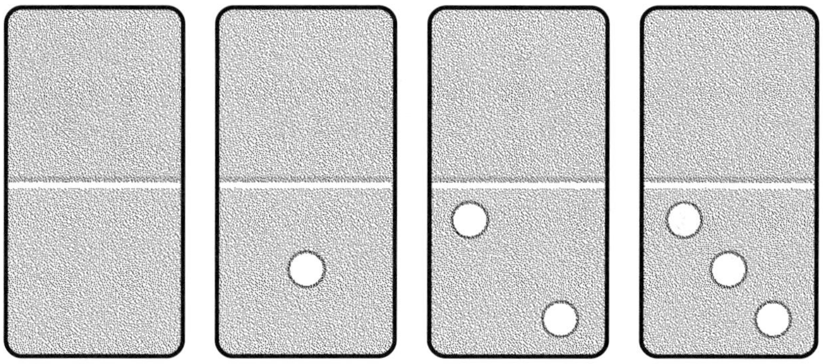

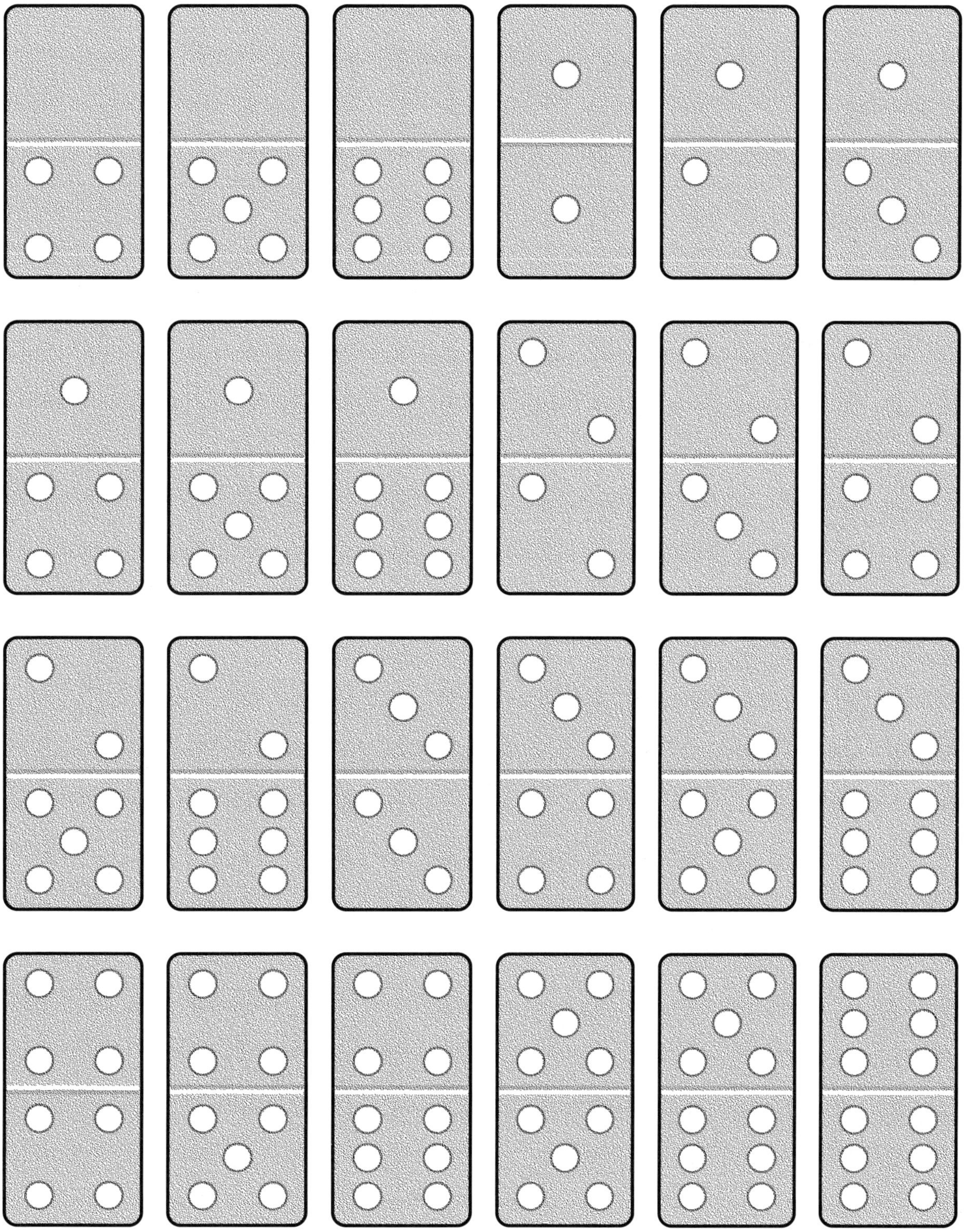

© Network Educational Press Ltd

© Network Educational Press Ltd

Tiles and string

Main focus

Searching for and describing patterns in results

Content

Relationship between areas and perimeters of rectangles, keeping one quantity fixed

Using the knowledge of factors to solve problems

Notes for teachers

Pupils' understanding of measures such as lengths, perimeters, areas and volume is greatly enhanced when they can practically explore the relationships between them.

It is important to offer pupils an opportunity to describe these relationships in their own words.

In both the activities pupils should be invited to talk and write about how the numbers in the tables relate to the problems.

Learning outcomes

The pupils are able to:

- make connections between arrangements of tiles and factors of the numbers involved;
- search for and describe patterns and relationships.

Evaluation

Could the pupils:

- complete all the different arrangement of tiles?
- record their results appropriately?
- make connections between the arrangements of tiles and numbers in the table?
- describe relationships in words?
- predict answers by spotting patterns?

Further activity

Square Tiles 2 can be extended by asking pupils to draw a graph of the width against length and comment on the symmetry. Pupils could investigate different arrangements of tiles keeping the perimeter fixed.

Resources

Pupil task sheets, cm^2 grid paper, dotted paper

© Network Educational Press Ltd

Square tiles 1

How many different rectangles can you make from square tiles?

For three tiles there is only one rectangle.

For four tiles you could make both of these. (*Remember:* a square is a special kind of rectangle.)

Try different numbers of tiles up to 16. Use cm^2 paper or dotted paper. Make a note of the lengths and widths of the rectangles.

Number of tiles	Number of different rectangles	Length, width
3	1	3,1
4	2	4,1 2,2
5		
6		
7		
8		
9		

Number of tiles	Number of different rectangles	Length, width
10		
11		
12		
13		
14		
15		
16		

If you have 24 tiles, can you work out how many different rectangles you could make without drawing them?

....

Explain how you would do it.

....

....

....

....

© Network Educational Press Ltd

Square tiles 2

You have a 36-centimetre piece of string and 1 cm^2 tiles.

You want to arrange the tiles in as many different rectangular shapes as possible using the 36 cm string to surround them.

17 cm

Using cm^2 paper, try to find all the possible rectangles.

Record your results in the table below.

36 cm string	
Rectangle	Tiles
17 × 1	17

Which rectangle contains the largest number of tiles?

....

What is special about it?

....

....

Try pieces of string 24 cm long and work out which rectangle will contain the most number of tiles.

....

Without drawing the tiles, work out the most number of tiles a 32 cm piece of string will surround.

....

© Network Educational Press Ltd

© Network Educational Press Ltd

© Network Educational Press Ltd

Mathematical understanding is improved when pupils' own experiences are used appropriately as a source of learning activities.

Do not always give pupils rules which work. Invite them to try some which do not, and say why they do not.
(See Unit 4 and Case Study on p. 103.)

© Network Educational Press Ltd

Appropriate approximations

Main focus

Rounding off sums of money using mental methods

Content

Approximating and adding sums of money mentally

Extracting relevant information from a given situation

Notes for teachers

Both the activities are designed to offer pupils experience of devising and practising quick ways of extracting information and calculating mentally.

In order to encourage pupils to think harder, the context chosen is not an 'everyday' one for them.

Discuss a few examples with the class to establish what constitutes a good strategy.

Encourage pupils to explain their methods.

Encourage pupils to discuss their work at home.

Learning outcomes

Pupils are able to:

- understand and apply mathematics to adult contexts;
- devise sensible and quick strategies for solving problems mentally.

Evaluation

Could the pupils:

- interpret the problems correctly?
- devise sensible methods of approximating?
- calculate mentally and obtain sensible answers?
- check their own answers using a reliable method?

Further activity

Ask pupils to bring examples of 'special offers' from newspapers, shops and junk-mail to work out the 'best buy'.

Resources

Copies of pupil task sheets

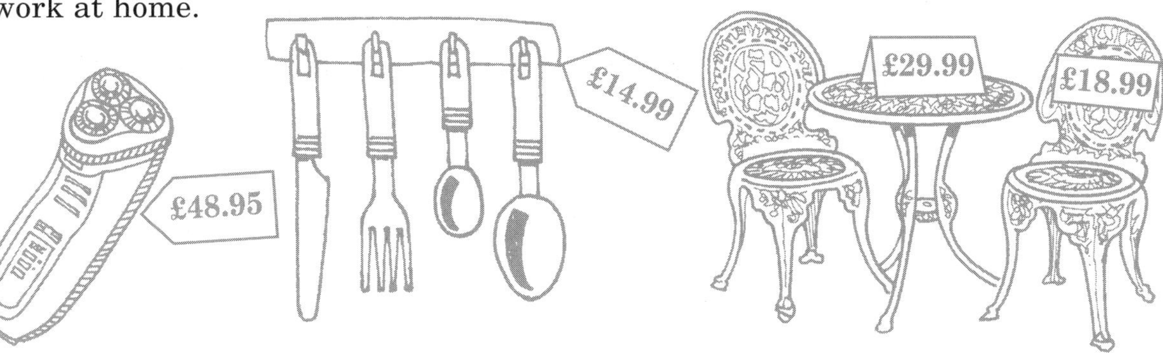

© Network Educational Press Ltd

Buy it all

Look at the following items.

This chart shows the amount you have to spend and in each case your aim is to spend as much as possible!

	I bought		I bought
£15		**£35**	
£80		**£210**	
£90		**£300**	
£140		**£420**	

Work out in your head which items you would buy. You can buy as many of each as you wish.

Write down the items you have bought for each amount.

Check your answers with a friend. Score 1 point for the best answer.

© Network Educational Press Ltd

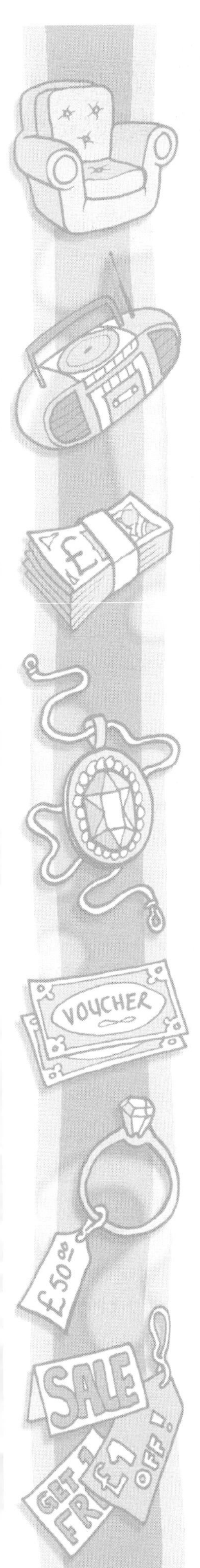

Buy it all

	I bought		I bought
£70		£400	
£160		£240	
£1000		£45	
£200		£100	
£25		£350	
£280		£360	
£500		£20	
£850		£50	
£700		£320	
£190		£650	
£900		£60	

© Network Educational Press Ltd

Bonus points

- 1 bonus point for every £10 spent
- For every 20 points collect a £2.50 voucher
- You can carry forward your points
- No bonus points on 'sale' goods

Look at the chart of goods bought by a family over 7 months.

Work out in your head how many bonus points have been collected each month. Now write them down in the table below.

January	
February	
March	
April	
May	
June	
July	

Write down how you worked out your answer.

....

....

....

....

....

Now check your answer. (Use a calculator if you wish.)

How many vouchers were collected by the end of July?

....

What was the total saving?

....

© Network Educational Press Ltd

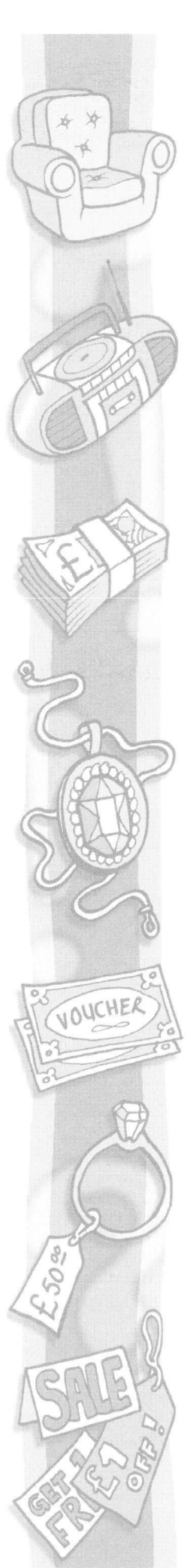

Bonus points

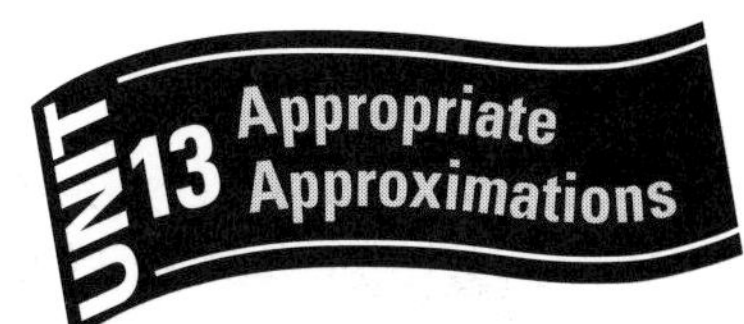

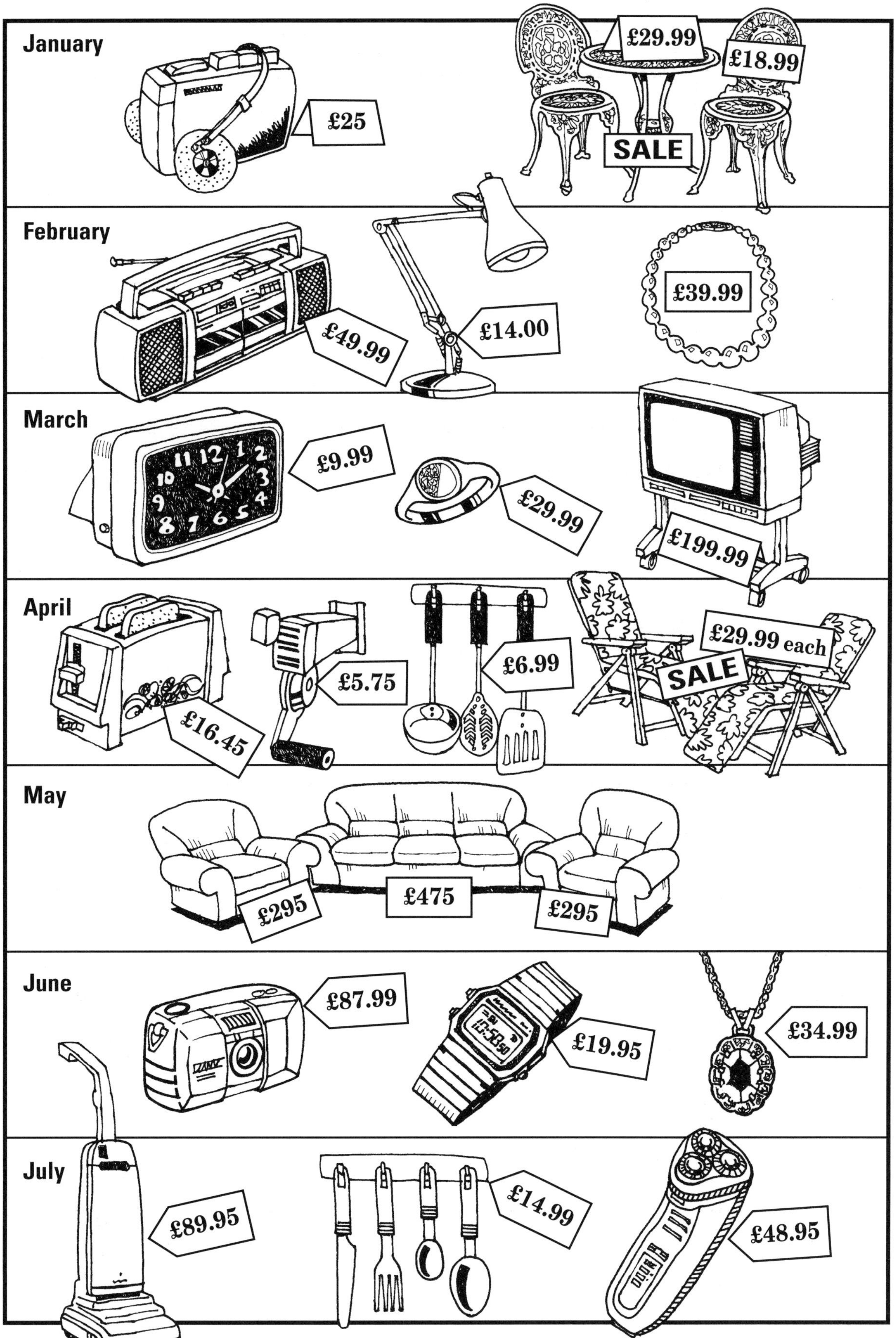

January
£25
£29.99
£18.99
SALE
February
£49.99
£14.00
£39.99
March
£9.99
£29.99
£199.99
April
£16.45
£5.75
£6.99
£29.99 each
SALE
May
£295
£475
£295
June
£87.99
£19.95
£34.99
July
£89.95
£14.99
£48.95

© Network Educational Press Ltd

Mathematical understanding is improved when imaginitive use is made of a wide variety of resources.

Show pupils examples of mistakes. Ask them to sort out what the mistakes are and to think how they might have arisen.

© Network Educational Press Ltd

Number machines

Main focus

Number relationships and functions

Content

Input/output and number 'machines' with three operations

Deducing relationships from number sentences

Notes for teachers

It is assumed that pupils have some experience of simple machines.

The first task sheet is designed to extend the knowledge of machines from two to three operations.

This kind of work is a good preparation for algebra and further work on functions (see Case Study). It is therefore important that pupils are helped to sharpen their descriptions and generalisations.

Learning outcomes

Pupils are able to:

- deal correctly with inputs and outputs involving three operations using simple numbers and fractions;
- deduce rules from number sentences.

Evaluation

Could the pupils:

- carry out calculations correctly?
- describe the number relationships unambiguously?

Further activity

Using the first task sheet, ask pupils to invent and solve word problems such as: 'If I have a number and I multiply it by 6, add 9 and divide by 3, I get 4. What number did I start with?'

Resources

Pupil task sheets

© Network Educational Press Ltd

Guess what the machine does?

When 3 goes into this machine, check that 4 comes out.

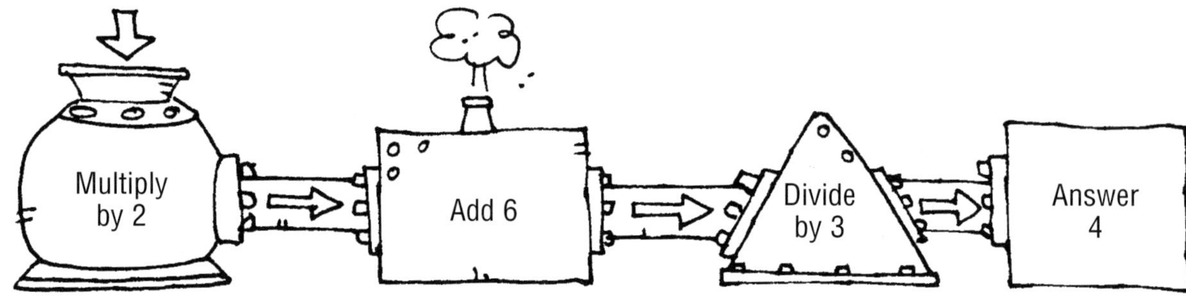

What happens to these numbers?

(a) 6 → ……… **(b) 12 →** ……… **(c) 1½ →** ……… **(d) 4½ →** ………

Now try this machine:

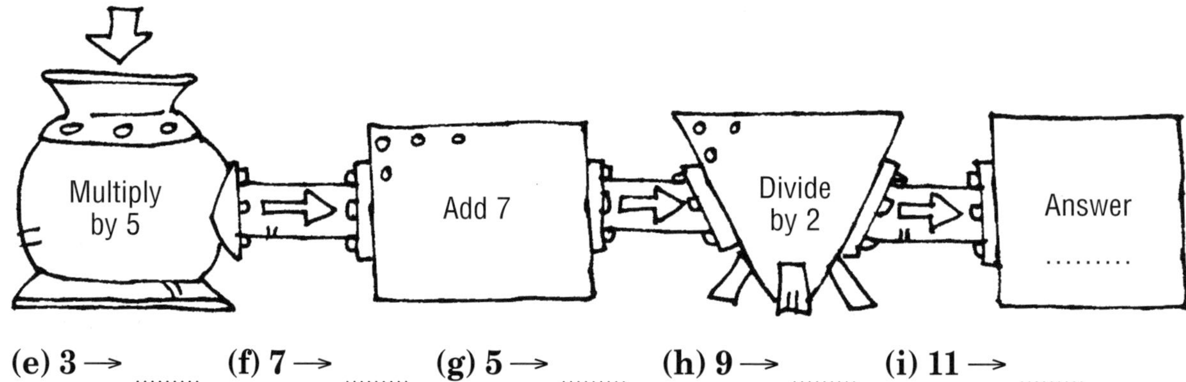

(e) 3 → ……… **(f) 7 →** ……… **(g) 5 →** ……… **(h) 9 →** ……… **(i) 11 →** ………

What happens when you put these numbers in the machine below?

(j) 10 → ……… **(k) 16 →** ……… **(l) 12 →** ……… **(m) 8 →** ……… **(n) 20 →** ………

Subtract 8

Multiply by 6

Divide by 4

Answer ………

© Network Educational Press Ltd

Guess what the machine does?

Now look at this one:

3 [○] 2 = 10

The machine [○] adds the two numbers and doubles the answer.

Try:

6 [○] 1 = ..., 9 [○] 1 = ..., 13 [○] 12 = ..., $1\frac{1}{2}$ [○] $2\frac{1}{2}$ = ...

Guess what the machines 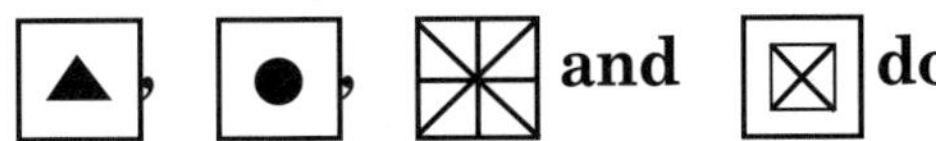 **and [⊠] do.**

A			**B**		
	3 [▲] 2 = 25			**3 [●] 9 = 12**	
	5 [▲] 1 = 36			**3 [●] 5 = 4**	
	7 [▲] 1 = 64			**5 [●] 12 = 14**	
	2 [▲] 2 = 16			**15 [●] 20 = 10**	(Try subtracting)

(Do the answers give you a clue?)

C		**D**	
	6 [✳] 1 = 70		**30 [⊠] 50 = 40**
	1 [✳] 1 = 20		**9 [⊠] 7 = 8**
	7 [✳] 3 = 100		**15 [⊠] 45 = 30**
	3 [✳] 3 = 60		**60 [⊠] 60 = 60**

A [▲] **stands for** ....
....
....

B [●] **stands for** ....
....
....

C [✳] **stands for** ....
....
....

D [⊠] **stands for** ....
....
....

© Network Educational Press Ltd

Recall of facts and speed in computation are improved when skills are sustained through meaningful practice and enjoyable drill.

Consider how you might incorporate the terms and notations that you want pupils to learn, so that meaning can be readily ascribed to them and they can be seen as helpful and necessary.

© Network Educational Press Ltd

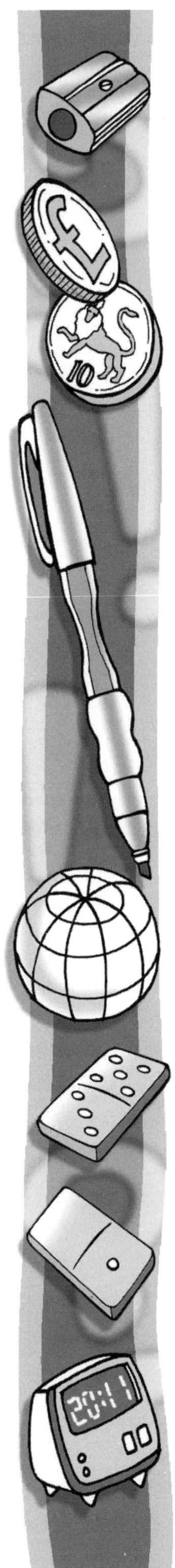

$n^2 - n + 11$

This extract is taken from Marion Bird's *Mathematics with Ten and Eleven Year Olds*, published by The Mathematical Association.

I showed the children $n^2 - n + 11$

I asked if anyone had any ideas about what this might be inviting us to do. They thought for a while, then Harvey suggested that perhaps 'n' meant 'a number' and we could choose one. Others seemed to think that this sounded sensible, so I asked them to choose a number, preferably quite small to start with, say under 10.

Madeline chose 6. I asked what we had to do first with the 6 and someone said that we had to multiply it by 6. Everyone agreed that that gave 36 and that next we had to subtract 6, then add 11. This gave 41 which, as a girl immediately pointed out, was a prime number.

I asked the children to make a note of the $n \times n - n + 11$ expression and of what happened when n equalled 6, and to try out other numbers for n. Mandy asked if they had to write 'n' or could they use other letters? I thought that she was thinking about heading her page with an expression such as $a \times a - a + 11$, with 'a' replacing 'n', and then trying out numbers for 'a'. I said that there was no need to keep to 'n'. I left the group.

On returning later, I found out that some of the children had been altering the letter with each number they tried out (the pupils' work enclosed gives an indication of this). I thought about commenting on this, but the children were so full of the things which they had noticed and of ideas to try out next, that I decided to leave raising the issue for the time being.

I listed the children's suggestions of other ideas on a piece of sugar-paper in front of them. This gave us:

- Larger numbers for n?
- Try different numbers instead of 11.
- Try different numbers when you are multiplying.
- Swop different parts round.
- Change signs.

There was no need to suggest that the children picked an idea to try, because they started doing so spontaneously!

© Network Educational Press Ltd

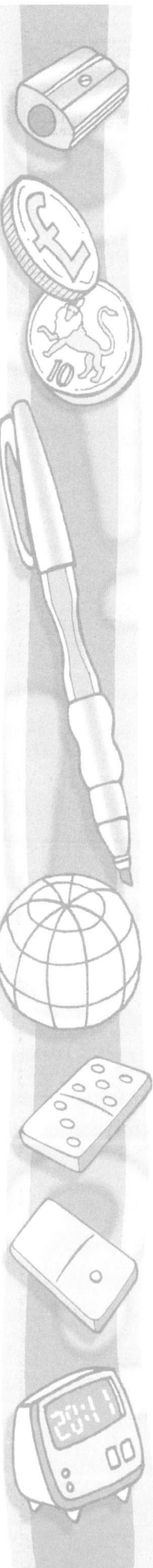

Penny's answer

n x n - n + 11

We chose 6 for our number to put insted of n then we x 6x6 and -6 and added 11. The answer was 41 which is a <u>prime</u> number.

P x P - P + 12

I chose 5 as my number to put insted of P. then I x 5x5 and -5 then + 12 the answer was 32 which isn't a prime number.

A x A - A + 2

I chose 3 as my number to put insted of A. I x 3x3 then I -3 then + 2. The answer was 8. 8 also is <u>not</u> a <u>prime</u> number because even numbers go into it.

u x u - u + 7

I chose 4 as my number insted of u. then I x 4x4 - 4 + 7. The answer was 19 which is a <u>prime</u> number.

Insted of using 11 to + or - on the end I changed the number each time I did a different sum.

© Network Educational Press Ltd

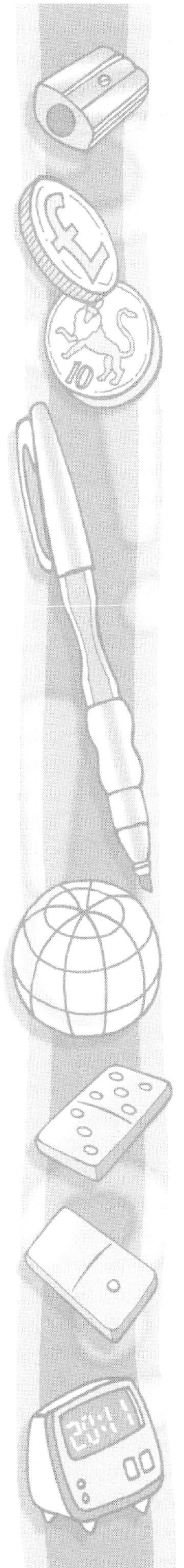

Simon's answer

$n \times n - n + 11 = 41$

This sum might seem silly at first because you think how are you ment to x n by n but if you think n could stand for number so chosse a number try under 10 like 6 so you put a sum like this $n \times n - n + 11 = 41$
$6 \times 6 - 6 + 11 = 41$
So most numbers under 10 = a prime number.

$B \times B - B + 11 = 23$

I chosse 4 so I x 4 by 4 − 4 + 11 and I got 23 which is a prime number. So I think that if you add an odd number on the end you get a prime number as an answer. If you add an even number on the end you get an even number as an answer.

$Z + 2 - Z + Z + 11 = 17$ ← Did you mean to change the form of what you have written here?

This time Z stands for 3 so again it is a prime number, and the sum is $3 + 3 - 3 + 3 + 11 = 17$.

$D + D - D + 11 = 31$

D stands for 5 so the sum is $5 + 5 - 5 + 11 = 31$ which is a prime number and every time you add 11 you get a prime number and if you add any other number you get an odd number and this is a thought but I am not positive that it is true.

© Network Educational Press Ltd

Multiplication grids

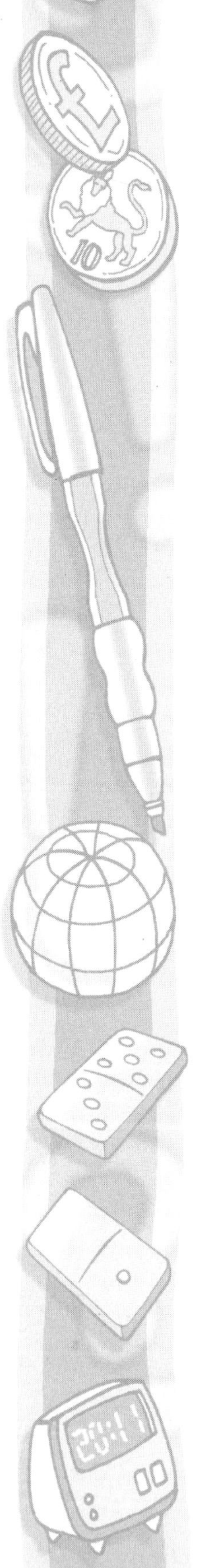

1	2	3	4	5	6	7	8	9	10	11	12
2	4	6	8	10	12	14	16	18	20	22	24
3	6	9	12	15	18	21	24	27	30	33	36
4	8	12	16	20	24	28	32	36	40	44	48
5	10	15	20	25	30	35	40	45	50	55	60
6	12	18	24	30	36	42	48	54	60	66	72
7	14	21	28	35	42	49	56	63	70	77	84
8	16	24	32	40	48	56	64	72	80	88	96
9	18	27	36	45	54	63	72	81	90	99	108
10	20	30	40	50	60	70	80	90	100	110	120
11	22	33	44	55	66	77	88	99	110	121	132
12	24	36	48	60	72	84	96	108	120	132	144

1	2	3	4	5	6	7	8	9	10	11	12
2	4	6	8	10	12	14	16	18	20	22	24
3	6	9	12	15	18	21	24	27	30	33	36
4	8	12	16	20	24	28	32	36	40	44	48
5	10	15	20	25	30	35	40	45	50	55	60
6	12	18	24	30	36	42	48	54	60	66	72
7	14	21	28	35	42	49	56	63	70	77	84
8	16	24	32	40	48	56	64	72	80	88	96
9	18	27	36	45	54	63	72	81	90	99	108
10	20	30	40	50	60	70	80	90	100	110	120
11	22	33	44	55	66	77	88	99	110	121	132
12	24	36	48	60	72	84	96	108	120	132	144

© Network Educational Press Ltd